THE FIVE WHOLENESS STEPS

God's Simple Plan for Healing the Wounded Soul

KATIE MATHER

BCR Press

The Five Wholeness Steps
By Katie Mather

www.BCRcamp.com

Published by BCR Press, an imprint of TrimVentures Publishing.
www.trimventures.com

ISBN-13: 978-0-9987415-9-8

Second Edition

DEDICATION

To Tim, my husband of these past forty years.
You showed me hope when I had none.
You believed in me when I didn't believe in myself.
Because of you, my life is changed. My heart is forever yours.

TABLE OF CONTENTS

Introduction

A Prodigal Son Moment

Most people don't do anything about their issues unless there is a crisis. We tend to stay right where we are, doing and believing the same things, unless there is a confrontation with the problem. The crisis then further escalates when change or resolution is necessary. Sometimes we may reach this point of revelation all by ourselves; oftentimes we come face-to-face with it during a conflict with someone else. Perhaps you are in one of these situations today. My hope is that there has been some kind of crisis that has forced you to take a good look at your life and do something about it.

The precursor to most personal change is what I like to call a "prodigal son" moment. In Luke 15:11-32, Jesus tells the story of a son who squandered his inheritance, then "came to himself" while starving and feeding someone's pigs. When he bottomed out and realized he didn't have to live like that, he humbled himself and returned home.

Just like the prodigal son, a lot of Christians have squandered their inheritance of the Kingdom and are living with less than all that Jesus has provided. Many people's lives are filled with crisis after crisis, each time giving us an opportunity to "come to ourselves" and return home to Father, but instead we try to pull it together and make it on our own. Broken hearts and bruised souls go ignored until we ultimately realize our need for a Savior.

In Luke 4:18, when He reads from the book of Isaiah, Jesus states that the anointing is on Him to declare the good news of the Kingdom, including healing for the broken hearted, freedom for the captives, liberty for the deeply bruised, and recovery of spiritual sight for the blind. Father has provided us with an inheritance of deliverance from the enemy who holds us captive to the lies in our own minds. He has made provision of inner healing for our wounded hearts and emotions. When we come to Christ and give our lives to Him, we are to come with all our emotional, intellectual, physical, and spiritual baggage. We do not need to be ashamed of our wounds nor hide our brokenness; we are to no longer believe those lies buried deep in our wounded souls.

How many times have we heard, "Isn't it great to be free?" But the church, the *ekklesia*, the "called out ones," are not free. We are called out of our brokenness, our wounds, and our bondage. We are called out of our unbelief and our distorted perceptions of ourselves and of Father. However, the church today is like the Laodicean church, claiming to be rich and have all it needs in pastors, buildings, programs, worship bands, and kids' ministries; but it is actually "wretched, poor, blind, and naked" because the individuals who make up the church do not admit to their wounds or confront the unbelief and lies within themselves.

George Barna is a Christian pollster who, over the years, has reported statistics on depression, divorce, sex and pornography addiction, anxiety, and drug and alcohol addiction in the church. His research has revealed only nine percent of all Americans have a biblical worldview. A biblical worldview is defined as believing the following: the existence of absolute moral truth; the complete accuracy of the Bible in all the principles it teaches; the reality of Satan as a being or force, not merely a symbol; entrance into heaven cannot be obtained through good behavior and/or good works; the sinless life of Jesus Christ on earth; and God as the all-knowing, all-powerful creator who still rules the universe today. Born again Christians are twice as likely as the average adult to possess a biblical worldview. However, that means even among born again Christians, less than one out of every five (nineteen percent) have such an outlook on life.

My husband, Tim, and I had a crisis one day in 1993 that changed our lives forever. As I look back, I can see how there were many events leading us up to that moment. God sometimes sets us up! Deliverance had removed the liars who infested my thinking and wounded heart, but I knew I still needed to confront the lies in my wounds that gave place to the enemy in order to be free and live according to my inheritance. I was lonely inside and full of self-loathing. There were dirty, evil thoughts that I couldn't control. I knew I was broken, but I didn't know how to fix myself. I had tried so hard to act like a Christian and perform for God in hopes that He would approve of me, but I would still feel so worthless inside. In this pigpen of mental and emotional garbage, I came to myself and realized my Father has plenty for me and, like the son in Jesus' parable, I needed to "come home."

Over twenty years ago, I took a risk and mustered all that I could and trusted Tim to listen to the Holy Spirit about how to heal me. It was not easy. It was downright difficult. I had spent over thirty-five years ignoring the pain and brokenness within myself. I was the queen of denial, ruling my own heart and keeping it imprisoned to never feel and never love. I was ignorant of the reality that my shame and my pain ruled me. In *The Five Wholeness Steps* I will share with you the journey of healing where Jesus took me by the hand and, together with my husband, we looked at the wounded places and the lies that I allowed to rule me.

My prayer is that you, too, will come to a place where you will open up your heart and allow the Savior in to cleanse, heal, and transform. Our Advanced Wholeness Retreat is designed to do that. You don't need to get stuck or plateau in your deliverance recovery to attend this retreat. The Advanced Wholeness Retreat will give you the opportunity to uncover the hidden places—the wounded places—that still rule you and keep you from your authentic self.

SECTION 1

AN OVERCOMER'S STORY

Chapter 1

THE ROAD TO DELIVERANCE

UNCOVERING THE UNEXPECTED

"I'll never tell you anything more about myself because you always hurt me with it!" I screamed as I leapt at Tim, balling up my fist, and splitting his lip. He stepped back for a moment with fire in his eyes. I swung again. This time he held up his arms to protect his face.

I was hot with anger as he demanded again and again, "What other secrets have you been keeping from me?"

Whenever I had reluctantly shared something of my past, it always came back to bite me as condemnation from him. I was fed up with the accusations of unfaithfulness. We had moved to a town close to where I grew up and it put a lot of pressure on our marriage. Now I exploded with rage from the judgment and accusation.

In the midst of my tirade, Tim appeared well-composed as he firmly commanded me to sit. *This is odd*, I thought as I sat down on the bed and folded my hands. He pressed the issue, "What other secrets have you kept from me?"

I thought for a moment and decided to hit him with my deepest, darkest secret. If I tell him this, he will see how truly evil I am.

"Did I ever tell you that I was sexually molested as a child?" I blurted. I awaited the barrage of accusations and condemnation, but it didn't come.

Instead, Tim fell against the wall, struck with an astonishing epiphany, exclaiming, "That's it! That explains everything. It all makes sense now!"

I had no idea what he meant. None of his reactions made sense to me.

Something changed in the atmosphere of the room. Because of Tim's reaction, I suddenly felt safe to share parts of my life that Tim had never known in our eighteen years of marriage. In the next several hours, I poured out the details of my childhood sexual abuse. I told him how, at the age of three, I was molested by a group of neighborhood boys; then from ages four to seven I was sexually abused by one of my mother's piano students. I confessed that ever since I was a child I thought this had happened to me because I was a nasty, bad person and, worst of all, I thought I had caused it to happen. I told my husband about the hurts of my parents' bad marriage and how, when I was only twelve years old, I attempted suicide.

For several months prior to this, I had been contemplating Prophetic Deliverance. I wrestled with some inner struggles. No matter how hard I tried I couldn't end the war within me. Now, with the exposure of these traumatic events in my life and the wounds they created, I was sure I needed deliverance.

HEY YOU, COME OUT OF THERE

Twelve years before this confrontation and confession, around the time Tim had gone through his own deliverance, an elder and his wife at our church prayed with me at the altar after a service. They identified something they called a spider and commanded it to leave. I wasn't sure what it meant, but for years after that I had assumed I was fully delivered. After all, I had been delivered of something. Looking back, I call that my, "Hey you, come out of there" deliverance. I was certain something had left me because I noticed some change in my life. Yet, I was not sure of what it was or what it was doing because it was not identified by its functional name. At least Tim knew he had been delivered of a spirit of fear.

Because it was not a Prophetic Deliverance and the chief demon was not identified, I remained demonized.

For many years after that experience, Tim often said he didn't believe I loved him. I knew something must be wrong with me. I realized if my husband didn't feel that I love him, what did my children feel? I also had many inner hateful, toxic thoughts running through my mind that couldn't be healed by reading my Bible more, praying more, or crying at the altar every Sunday. No amount of religious performance could erase my feelings of absolute evilness and shame.

We both agreed I needed Prophetic Deliverance.

THE LAST DELIVERANCE

A few days later, we were on our way to a conference with Tim's parents. As we traveled, Tim asked his folks, Pastor Fran and Shirley Mather, if they would take me through deliverance after the evening service that night. During that service, there was a lot of demonic activity causing friction between Tim and me that set a stage for conflict once again. When we got back to the hotel room, Tim asked his dad to lead the deliverance session while he observed. He informed us that he had a list of the demons' names and would sit by to make sure they were all identified.

Pastor Fran had been through Tim's deliverance training and had done many Prophetic Deliverance sessions before, but he felt uncomfortable without Tim's participation. I felt some sense of relief to have Shirley there because I knew Tim had received his mom's acute spiritual gifting. I was sure she would see and hear what was going on with me.

As the session began, Fran identified a specific spirit but refused to name it. I kept thinking, *Please just say it*. Somehow, I knew what he would say. He finally gave in and declared, "Spirit of whoredom." I thought, *Whew, finally!* Later he told me that he was concerned I would jump up and punch him in the lip, too.

Fran also felt the Lord showed him how that spirit would talk to others about me. Today, we call that a sex-based control spirit. (To learn more about control spirits, see Tim's book *Out of Bondage*.) He described how I was faithful to Tim our whole marriage, but this spirit would tell Tim that I was not. It was active in convincing Tim that I was an unfaithful wife. Thus our marriage was full of suspicion and accusation.

A spirit of "perfectionism" was named, which confused me. I thought it was good to have high standards. A spirit of "deception" and a few others were named, but then Fran paused. Shirley could see into the spirit realm, a demon hiding deep within me. As soon as she saw this, I started to feel something move in my body and it became difficult to breathe. I felt as though I was being choked from the inside out, as if something held on to me and refused to let go.

They had difficulty identifying its functional name. Tim, frantic that I might not survive, asked his dad to have the demon reveal its name. I heard this word deep in my mind, but because we don't allow demons to speak or manifest, I didn't know what to do. I opened my mouth to speak the word and even though I heard my own little voice, Tim and his parents heard an otherworldly voice growl, "I am control!" They commanded the control spirit to leave, along with all others under its authority, and immediately began to pray healing for my wounded spirit.

THE POST-TEST

I spent most of that night weeping in the bathroom of our hotel room, not sure of what had happened. Tim wasn't too sure either. He knew how I could play the role and appear changed, so he challenged me with a test. Tim wanted a sign to confirm my deliverance. He told me that if I did this specific task that only he and God knew about, then he would know the deliverance was real.

Tim had played mind games with me all of our married life, but now I had no idea what to do. I was scared. So I wept before Father and begged Him to show me. When Tim came into the bathroom, I told him the only thing I could think of: I was to wash his feet. Doubt still covered his face. I knew foot washing could be perceived as more of my religious performance and I feared I was wrong. I poured water over his feet into a basin. I rubbed them and proceeded to do something out of character. I was all in, so I even washed between his toes. At that moment, he became overjoyed. The specific thing he wanted me to do to prove my deliverance was real was to not only wash his feet but also between his toes—something I wouldn't normally do.

The next morning, we gathered for breakfast. In the hotel restaurant, I started to weep over my eggs. I blubbered, "I've never eaten eggs without demons before!" In that moment I realized it felt like I had lived with a screen mesh, like a fencing mask, over my face. Everything I perceived in life had been strained through it.

My world already started to feel cleaner.

A MEMORIAL TO GOD'S PROMISE

Later in the day, while sitting in one of the workshops at the conference, the speaker shared how the children of Israel would place a pile of stones in the wilderness where they traveled as a reminder of the mighty things God had done for them. I elbowed Tim and said, "Maybe we should pile some rocks in our hotel room." He immediately handed me his notebook where he had already written, "As a reminder of the mighty thing I am doing in your wife's life, call her Katie."

My legal name is Kathleen and I had gone by "Kathy" until that moment. At the time, I had no clue as to what the "mighty thing" God would do in my life. I have been Katie ever since, not because Katie meant anything better than Kathy, but that every time I heard Katie I would remember and be encouraged by His promise.

THE PROCESS BEGAN

As soon as we got home, we called a family meeting. At the time, our children were ages seventeen, sixteen, fourteen, and twelve. We sat them down and told them everything: the fight, the confession about the abuse, and the deliverance. In the weeks that followed, Tim and I spent many hours every day working on peeling back the layers of coping mechanisms, beliefs and behaviors that blanketed my deep, life-long wounds. Tim was intent upon finding the woman he knew was in there somewhere. I was frightened, and I felt vulnerable. I didn't know who I was anymore. I clung to the promise that God would do a "mighty thing" and desperately hoped He would show Tim how to heal me.

Chapter 2

Journey Through the Wounds

Fear of Exposure

The first Sunday we were back in church after the deliverance, I hid in the side room before the service. I was weeping, having a panic attack. Tim found me and asked me what was going on. All I could get out was I was too afraid to face those people. Me? Afraid?

I had never been afraid of anything in my whole life. I had played drums and sung on worship teams for many years in ministry. I used to be able to do anything and speak to anyone, but now I felt exposed and naked to the world. Nobody knew what had happened the week before—only Tim's parents, with whom we co-pastored, and our children. I was afraid people could see my brokenness, my "dirtiness." I was free of demons, but I still needed healing. I felt my wounded soul showed.

Before we married, Tim and I had dated for three years. Those were troubling years for both of us. We fought all the time. It was a miracle we stayed together or married. I didn't only struggle with the relationship with Tim, but also struggled to put my past life behind me and live for Jesus. I always felt I had failed greatly in both relationships.

Soon after, it was May—the month of our wedding anniversary. In expectation of the mighty thing God said He would do in me, we decided to renew our wedding vows, this time using my new name, Katie. After a small family gathering where we shared new promises and a new spark of love in our marriage, we left for Virginia Beach. It was where we had spent our original honeymoon. We got away to discover each other once again.

On the way, we stopped to see my mother. She had an odd reaction to seeing me for the first time after deliverance. In the parking lot of the restaurant where we met for lunch, she called out, "What is the matter with you?" I knew my mother could not see me from that distance without her glasses, but something in her knew I was different. After we ate and got back to her house, we told her the story of the argument that led to the divulged secret and the deliverance with Tim's folks. Since this was way off the radar of my mother's experience as a devoted Methodist, all she could understand was I was hurt inside.

UNCOVERING WOUNDS

During the entire car ride down and back from Virginia Beach, Tim was filled with questions. I tried to answer the best I could. For the most part, I felt like I was under an interrogation light. Tim was intent on finding out what, where, who, and why, not only about the abuse, but also about any and every detail of my life.

It was painful.

I could not see it at the time, but Tim was trying to peel back the layers of protection and denial I had built around myself. It was like a wall of smoke and mirrors to divert attention and hide my wounded self. As a child, I had lived in deception. I was never to tell anyone about what I saw and heard at home. Even my abusers made me promise never to tell anyone about our "secret." Therefore, I held my abuses and secrets within me, as in a deep, dark cavern. The way I saw it, I hadn't been lying to Tim—I just hadn't told him the whole truth.

FULL DISCLOSURE AGREEMENTS

I made many agreements with Tim as I began to understand his reason for searching through my past to find the wounds that needed healing. The first agreement was to not keep secrets. Any secret. If I ever felt I was keeping a secret, I had to tell him even if it was how much I spent at a rummage sale. This was to break free of the lie of feeling safe in deception and secrets. I needed to feel safe in our relationship, not in my secrets.

This not only granted me a place of safety but brought resolution to many confusing issues about me in Tim's mind. Over the eighteen years of our marriage and the three years of dating, Tim's imagination (and the input from the demons) had created a world where I had been an unfaithful wife. He looked for every bit of information to put to rest these thoughts.

The second major agreement was to stop avoiding the fear of exposure. Tim had been a Security Policeman in the Air Force, and he was proficient in interrogation techniques. However, when he asked me a "who, what, when, where, why" question, if I could not answer, I couldn't say, "I don't know" but rather, "I will think about it" and get back to him on it. That was because I *did* know. I had buried what I thought and believed deep in my unconscious mind. I covered it with denial to try to protect my painful wounds. When I took the time to think each time a question was asked, I would bravely look past my denial to find the answer. This exercise helped me to break through my protective denial to discover the wounds that needed to be found, revealed, and discussed to begin healing in that area.

Another big agreement I made with Tim was to stop controlling. I needed to learn that my efforts to control were rooted in my inability to trust. Control damages all relationships, especially the relationship with the Father. The person who is addicted to control is one who is controlled by fear. In order to heal, I had to face what was behind my need to control, my fear of being controlled, and my fear of being hurt. This didn't mean

I came under Tim's control, but rather I had to be accountable and self-aware as to when my need to control flared up. At first it was hard because I didn't recognize I was being controlling. Of course, I needed Tim to tell me how and when I controlled. I knew this was especially important because the chief demon I was delivered from was "control," and I did not want to leave any door or window open even one little crack for the enemy to come back. I desperately wanted to be free, especially free to know how to love, not control.

INNER HEALING ASSIGNMENTS

When we returned from our honeymoon trip to Virginia Beach, we told our children that if our bedroom door was closed, we were working on healing me and were not to be disturbed. Over the next few months, Tim and I spent at least four to six hours every day working on "inner healing stuff."

In between sessions, as an inner healing assignment, I had to think of the reasons "why I did what I did" and "why I thought what I thought" on certain topics. It was difficult recalling the "why's" of my life; it was even more difficult to communicate my thoughts and feelings, simply because I had never communicated on that level before.

Most of the time, I wept my way through the sessions. My brain would hurt as though I had taken an exam in school. The emotional pain we uncovered felt excruciating. I felt all the shame of my life lay exposed and dissected, like on a coroner's table, as we worked through my broken soul.

HUNT FOR HEALING RESOURCES

I also became hungry to find resources that would lead me to God's healing. I first found David Seamands' books. In *Healing for Damaged Emotions*, I read about how God cares about our wounded emotions. Seamands also pinpointed the issues of perfectionism and guided me to the Father's answer: grace. His

Freedom from the Performance Trap showed me more about the miracle of grace and how my performance-driven personality needed healing. In his *Putting Away Childish Things*, I saw how I was stuck in the traumas of my childhood. Seamands' *Healing of Memories* told me about the healing power of the Spirit for emotional pain.

Because I was ignorant of the effects of childhood sexual abuse, I began searching for books on recovery for Christians. I wanted to find out what happens to a person who has been abused. Some recovery materials talked only about being a survivor, but I didn't want to be labeled a survivor. I wanted to heal and be free of the effects of the victimization. When I saw the list of characteristics of abuse victims in Cindy Kubetin's book, *Beyond the Darkness: Healing for Victims of Childhood Sexual Abuse*, I knew I had found gold. From a list of twenty-five signs and symptoms, I had all of them except one. She also talked about not being a survivor of childhood sexual abuse, but an overcomer. That is what I wanted! Like it says in Revelation:

> *He who has an ear, let him hear what the Spirit says to the churches. To him who overcomes I will give some of the hidden manna to eat. And I will give him a white stone, and on the stone a new name written which no one knows except him who receives it.*
> Revelation 2:17, NKJV

My childhood was terribly painful, not only because of the sexual abuse, but because of the constant fighting between my parents. My three younger brothers and I were also traumatized because of our mother's abandonment. Working through healing meant processing those buried feelings of abandonment, as well as the hurt and anger from those deep wounds. The best recovery material I found on the topic of healing from the wounds of dysfunctional families was a book that outlines the characteristics of a dysfunctional family and how it ingrains a shame-based identity. I could see how shame was intertwined in my life through the shame of my mother's affairs. People would say to me how much I was like my mother (because we were both musical). All I could see was how shameful I was because of how promiscuous I was by the age of thirteen.

ACCUSATION VS. DISCOVERY

Often the hours Tim and I spent digging around in my past felt like going through surgery. Rather than an interrogation to accuse me, the process became more like a journey to discover what damage the traumas of my life had caused. One time I cried out, "Why do we always have to go digging around in the crap of my life?"

Tim replied, "Every once in a while, we discover a gem under the crap."

Personally, all I could see was crap, but Tim saw more of the true person inside.

Working her way to the surface was a deeply wounded woman ruled by fear. To me this was odd because one of my protective coping mechanisms was a no-fear persona. I had never experienced a panic attack until after deliverance. I lived in so much denial of the wounds I carried that in order to heal, I needed to see the severely wounded person I was. I discovered how I needed to surrender my self-protection and coping behaviors to the Lord so I could experience His healing.

At first the process felt like little baby steps of surrender. However, the more I surrendered my brokenness to the Father's loving care, the more I experienced His healing. The more I healed, the more I realized I experienced Him, His presence, His essence, His healing love. The Creator of the universe revealed Himself to me as I laid down my self-judgments, my self-hatred, and my self-condemnation.

Chapter 3

PATH TO RESTORATION

POWER THROUGH EXPOSURE

About a month after my deliverance, Tim and I decided it was time to share with our church what was happening in my life. Several people noticed the change in me. I was much more subdued, often quiet, and acting quite insecure. There were intentional changes I made in my controlling behavior, along with changes I was experiencing as my soul healed.

That morning, before we left for church, I told Tim how scared I was to tell others about my secret, my life, and my shame. He told me a way to have power over this secret pain is to expose it. We prayed together, I took a deep breath, and we drove to church.

Tim titled his sermon "Freedom from the Bondage of Shame." We felt "shame" was the most profound discovery we had made so far in this healing journey. To illustrate the power of shame, I wore handcuffs throughout the service. I did all my church duties that morning and even sang on the worship team while in handcuffs. All through the service, the key to the handcuffs was taped to the overhead projector which could be seen on the projector screen on the wall.

Before Tim began to share, we asked all children to be

dismissed to children's church. With only the adults present, Tim revealed everything, including the fight, the confession of sexual abuse, the deliverance, and the inner healing work we had done thus far. He talked about how the key to healing had been there the whole time. (In the next chapter I will share what the key was and the role it played in the journey toward healing.)

As Tim took the key to unlock my handcuffs, his parents sang that old Bill Gaither song, "Shackled by a heavy burden, 'neath a load of guilt and shame. Then the hand of Jesus touched me and now I am no longer the same…" They barely got through the song before the whole room was teary-eyed.

Tim closed his message with an invitation. He invited anyone whose life had personally been touched by the destruction of childhood sexual abuse to step forward for prayer and make a commitment to begin the healing journey to freedom. Seventy five percent of the adults present stepped forward. On the cassette tape recording of that message, you can still hear Tim whispering under his breath, "Oh Lord, what are we going to do now?"

COMFORT WITH THE COMFORT YOU'VE BEEN COMFORTED WITH

We prayed with each one who came forward that day, but it took us several months to take all the people through Prophetic Deliverance and start them on their healing journey. We started small home groups for post-deliverance recovery using Robert McGee's excellent material, *The Search for Significance*. Although it is not designed for post-deliverance inner healing, it is thorough in confronting our faulty thinking and facilitating transformation. I had used *The Search for Significance* in my own recovery and found it most helpful in confronting my web of denial and exposing the lies I believed. It helped me find my identity and significance in God's truth about me instead of basing my worth in what other people say and do.

I also started a support group for women who were victims

of childhood sexual abuse and called it Overcomers, using Cindy Kubetin's book, *Beyond the Darkness*.

No Stone Unturned

Tim and I still worked on me every day, but I also shared the inner healing journey with many others in the support groups. The first women's group pressed me to heal even more. Father God showed me I could leave no stone unturned in my own life because I could not take others where I had not been myself. I was utterly dependent upon the Holy Spirit's guidance as I worked with the broken and wounded.

I had never before worked in this area of church ministry. Prior to deliverance I was not equipped to encounter the deep wounds of people's lives. I still felt ill-equipped after my deliverance, but I made myself available to share God's healing work and the journey to freedom that I experienced. I strained to hear His directions on how to guide people to this deep inner healing and blazed a path of inner healing for each person I would encounter from then on.

An End to Spiritual Abuse

I knew much of the pain I carried was from my childhood experiences with my family. As I studied the dysfunctional family, its characteristics and effects, I realized the church is a big dysfunctional family! I began to see many abuses in the church system and recognized much of what we did in ministry was actually abusive. I found many good resources describing spiritual abuse. One doesn't have to be a part of a cult in Waco or drink red Kool-Aid to experience spiritual abuse. As there is dysfunction in every earthly family, there is the dysfunction of spiritual abuse in every church.

In *The Subtle Power of Spiritual Abuse*, authors Johnson and Van Vonderen define spiritual abuse as denying a person spiritual empowerment. In Ephesians 4, Paul writes that apostles, prophets, evangelists, pastors, and teachers are gifts to the church to equip and empower believers to be mature in Christ. Realizing this changed our view on church and ministry. We gravitated toward the effectiveness of small groups gathering in homes and focused on empowering and equipping others.

FINDING HIS HEALING PRESENCE

About eight months into my healing journey, Tim and I, along with Tim's parents, took a trip to Lakeland, Florida to see Rodney Howard Browne. We heard the Holy Spirit "manifested" there and we wanted to investigate. It was quite a sight to see all the shaking and laughing. We would try to arrive early to sit as far forward as possible to get into the "flow." We finally arrived early enough to be seated about five rows from the front. Tim's Mom, Dad, Tim, and I squeezed into a four-seat pew. While we stood in worship, some guy slithered in between us, so when it came time to sit down, our five butts did not fit in a four-butt pew. Tim and I went to try to find a seat, but by that time the floor of the ten-thousand seat auditorium was full, and we were resigned to sit in the balcony.

I burned with anger, feeling left out and abandoned again. All my inner thoughts and my negative self-programming came right up to the surface. As the service came to a close, I saw those people down front get touched by the presence of the Holy Spirit. I saw an elegantly dressed woman jump into the aisle and dance to the Lord with abandonment. I wept bitterly as I envied her freedom and joy. I realized I still had a long way to go in my healing journey.

When we got home, we shared what had happened in Lakeland with our church, and renewal broke out in our fellowship that morning. The presence of the Holy Spirit was so strong that for sixteen consecutive weeks we didn't know what would happen on Sunday mornings. God's presence healed the broken and filled hungry hearts, mine included.

Several months later, when we heard about the Toronto

Outpouring, we went to see what the Lord was doing. In one of the services I went forward, but I was astonished to see and hear things that were definitely not caused by the Holy Spirit. The Lord helped me understand it was not the Holy Spirit causing people to make animal sounds, laugh, shake, and roll. Two factors were at play: first, it was the human soul and body's reaction to the intensity of the Holy Spirit's presence. For example, imagine how your body would react if you grabbed a live electric wire or got a jolt from a Taser. The second factor that made the people do odd things in the intense presence of the Holy Spirit was the presence of the demons on the person. In those early days, the Toronto group did not know what to do about the manifestation of those demons.

Back at home, to have the freedom to worship without the time constraints of Sunday morning, we developed an informal worship time on Friday nights and called it Friday Night Fire. The Holy Spirit's presence would heal and soothe those who were working on their wounds in the small home groups. The word began to get out that deliverance, healing, and the presence of the Holy Spirit were in our midst. I facilitated support groups and counseled people one-on-one for pre- and post-deliverance care. Our deliverance and inner healing ministry began to grow like a snowball rolling downhill.

WORTHY OF AN EDUCATION

I could feel the Lord telling me there was more He had for me. To put away childish things and conquer some inner vows, I needed to go to college. I had never been to college. Before deliverance I believed I was not worth the money or the time for college. So, at the age of thirty-eight, I enrolled in the local community college as a full-time student.

First, I received an Associate Degree in Social Services. Then, I went on to achieve a Bachelor of Science degree in Pastoral Counseling from Oral Roberts University. In 2006 I earned my Master of Ministry. Finally, in 2008, I received my

Doctor of Ministry with my dissertation on The Work of Inner Healing.

All while I worked on my Associate and Bachelor's degrees, I worked with people in pre- and post-deliverance counseling. I learned much from the Holy Spirit as I intently listened to His direction. While working on the many counseling courses from ORU, I was hoping to learn about the supernatural aspects of inner healing. Never once did any of my professors at ORU ever mention, define, or identify the supernatural component of the healing of the Holy Spirit in inner healing.

I made that the research topic for my Master's project. I studied several inner healing ministries to identify the common thread of the supernatural work of the Holy Spirit. Many ministries employed a "tossed salad" approach to Christianize psychology, but some of them actually accessed the healing work of the Holy Spirit to heal the wounds of the soul.

I also compared ministries to see which deliverance ministries believed in inner healing and which inner healing ministries utilized deliverance. Of all the ministries I studied back in the 90's, not one subscribed to the idea that people must receive deliverance first and then work on letting in the Holy Spirit to heal their wounds. This is still true today as we minister to the broken, wounded souls who come to us after seeking wholeness through other inner healing ministries.

DISCOVERIES OF GOD'S PATTERNS

I see from the pattern of Jesus' ministry that He delivered and healed those who came to Him. Then they followed Him and heard His teachings on the Kingdom. The rest of my story speaks of my discoveries of God's pattern for deliverance and inner healing. Yes, in that order.

This may be speculation, but I can't help but wonder if the Apostle Paul experienced deliverance from Jesus, Himself, because his letters are full of directions for healing the wounded soul. What a powerful transformation must have occurred in Paul's life to go from a self-righteous Pharisee who killed Christ's followers, to His greatest Apostle!

If you haven't already, you can read more about deliverance in Tim's book, *Prophetic Deliverance: The Missing Ministry of Jesus in the Church.*

DELIVERANCE FIRST

The story of the Gaderene demoniac shows us a pattern for deliverance as a prophetic ministry. Even though the man was severely demonized, he had the wherewithal to come towards Jesus. The King James Version uses the word "possessed" to describe this man's condition. However, if the man were actually "possessed" of a demon, so as to be entirely controlled by it, he would have been prevented from approaching Jesus. As we see in word study, the better translation is "demonization," meaning "afflicted by demons."

Jesus identified the ruling spirit as Legion, representing the thousands of demons infesting the man. This does not lead us to speak to demons or allow them to speak to us through the person. As Christ Himself commanded the demon to identify itself, we communicate with the *Holy Spirit of Christ* only. He communicates to us the functional name of the "strong man," or as we call it, the chief or ruling spirit. Once the strong man or ruling spirit is identified, then the house can be ransacked. As with the Gaderene demoniac, deliverance is more thorough and less time-consuming as the whole entourage is commanded to leave *en masse.*

I, like so many Christians, struggled my whole Christian walk to change myself. Jesus said, *"The thief comes only to steal and kill and destroy; I have come that they may have life, and have it to the full"* (John 10:10). Trying to pursue His abundant life while still demonized is like taking three steps forward and two steps back. The plan of the enemy as described in John 10:10 is to steal, kill, and destroy. Deliverance removes the presence of the enemy working against us. That is why deliverance is like spiritual surgery to remove the foreign object or cancerous tumor. After deliverance, a person needs to heal—and can heal—much more simply and deeply than before deliverance. Certainly, the healing Kingdom principles that I'm going to share with you can work and make a difference before Deliverance because they are His Kingdom truths. You will find, as many others have, His Healing will be more effective and go much deeper after the ministry of Prophetic Deliverance.

HEALING

The Healing Path I share with you is the transformational journey one can pursue after receiving deliverance. As I look back, my journey was painful and difficult, messy and disjointed. I didn't have anyone to show me how to heal. It was painful because I did not know how to trust. I struggled with the fear that Tim would turn on me and condemn me for what was buried inside. I knew Tim could hear from God, and with mustard seed-sized faith I clung to the hope my Heavenly Father would show him how to help me heal.

Looking back, I can see there was a path, and the Father guided me all along the way. It was difficult because all my survival mechanisms wanted to resist dying to the lies I believed, even though I knew there was life on the other side of surrendering those lies. It was messy because I had no one to come alongside to show me how simple healing is, to give me hope I would change and find that abundant life that Jesus talked about. Because I wanted it more than life itself, I pushed through the fear of the unknown and the pain of resistance and found Him, the Healer of my Wounded Soul.

JOURNEY OF ADVENTURE AND INTRIGUE

What you will find in the pages to come is the path I discovered while pursuing the healing my soul craved. As I have worked with hundreds of others, the Father has shown me how to guide people on His healing path. This is a journey of adventure, mystery, and intrigue. You will discover wounds long buried and hidden. You will find the lies in your soul that need to be discarded. Most of all, you will find the true treasure of yourself as you look into the face of the Father and He reflects back to you the true creation He designed you to be.

Have you been through Prophetic Deliverance? Now see what lies ahead!

SECTION 2

The Foundation of Inner Healing

Chapter 4

THE KEY

*The Spirit of the Lord is upon me, because he hath
anointed me to preach the gospel to the poor; he
hath sent me to heal the brokenhearted, to preach
deliverance to the captives, and recovering of sight
to the blind, to set at liberty them that are bruised, to
preach the acceptable year of the Lord.*
Luke 4:18-19, KJV

As I shared in the previous chapter, Tim shared *the key* to
my shackles during his Sunday morning sermon. My Prophetic
Deliverance and Inner Healing journey was *my story*, but Luke
4:18-19 was *the key* we presented as the answer, Father's answer,
to a multitude of age-old questions: "What is the purpose of life?
Why am I here? Who am I? Why all the suffering? What? Why?
Who?"

Jesus went into the desert and for forty days was tempted by
the devil. He returned in the power of the Holy Spirit and, in a
synagogue in Nazareth, He read from the scroll of Isaiah: *"The
Spirit of the Lord is on me."* Then, He said to them, *"Today this
scripture is fulfilled in your hearing"* (Luke 4:21).

Jesus made a declaration not only of His mission and His
purpose, but also of who He is as the answer to all our suffering.
In the reading of that scripture, He simply declared, "I'm here

to deliver you and heal your broken soul. I am here to open your eyes and show you who you are. I'm here to show you the Kingdom." It is not only Jesus' mission statement for His earthly ministry, but also for the entire ministry of His body, the church.

A mission statement is a summary of the purpose of an organization. I have seen this passage used by many ministries as their mission statement, but not to the fullness of ministering deliverance from demonization and presenting the pursuit of deep inner healing to the wounded soul. Let's take a closer look at what Jesus actually said in each section of this scripture.

THE SPIRIT OF THE LORD IS UPON ME...

Jesus was anointed with the Holy Spirit. When John baptized Him in the Jordan River, the Holy Spirit came upon Him. Then, throughout the gospels, Jesus is referred to as being "in the Spirit," and "full of the Holy Spirit." Often this "empowering" or "infilling" of the Holy Spirit as another work of grace is neglected, rejected, and even avoided among His Body today. Even Jesus gave Himself to be filled with the Holy Spirit.

Many Christians don't understand that the Holy Spirit will never violate our will. If we choose to only receive Jesus as Savior, and disregard the Holy Spirit's baptism of power, then we get what we have chosen.

Jesus imparted His Holy Spirit to those in the upper room who waited upon the promised arrival. They were then empowered with great boldness to share the stories of Jesus and to do the supernatural things that Jesus did. They also shared this with many other believers who had not yet received the Holy Spirit upon believing in Jesus. At salvation, we receive Jesus Christ as our Savior and the Holy Spirit is with us. We also need to seek to be filled and empowered by the Holy Spirit.

...BECAUSE HE HATH ANOINTED ME TO PREACH GOOD NEWS...

This anointing of the Holy Spirit was an empowerment to

"preach the good news." So what does it mean to preach? Today, this word brings up a certain image in our heads of a preacher, a pulpit, and a sermon. In its original context, "to preach" simply meant "to proclaim, to declare, to say." Preaching, therefore, is not limited to those who designate themselves as official proclaimers or preachers. We are *all* to share the good news.

This does not mean that next Sunday you should rush the pulpit, hip check the minister, and declare, "I've got something to preach!" No, this means in everyday life, simply share your good news. If you found eating a certain food made you lose all that extra weight and you had the energy of an 18-year-old, that would be good news! If you suddenly discovered a gas station selling gas at a dollar per gallon, you would tell everyone you know, right? That would certainly be good news.

So that brings us to the next question. What exactly *is* the good news that Jesus was talking about?

We were trained in Sunday school that the good news is the gospel, the story of Jesus recorded in Matthew, Mark, Luke, and John. Right? Jesus talked about Himself privately to His disciples, but He did not proclaim Himself as the good news. Jesus isn't the good news? We have somehow made the good news the story of His birth, life and death. We have made it about blood, a cross, and nails. "Jesus died for you so you could go to heaven!" That is all good and true, but Jesus knew people need good news for life right now.

After His declaration in the synagogue in Nazareth, Matthew 4:17 says, *"From that time on Jesus began to preach, 'Repent, for the kingdom of heaven has come near.'"* The good news is about the Kingdom of heaven. Jesus' parables were about the Kingdom. The Kingdom is like a seed, like a fishing net, like a treasure. When Jesus was confronted about casting out demons, Jesus replied, *"But if I drive out demons by the spirit of God, then the kingdom of God has come upon you"* (Matthew 12:28). The Kingdom that Jesus taught is not a life after death, but it is a Kingdom life right here and now that He brought with Him and demonstrated through His life and miracles.

I rarely use the word "repent" because of its misuse. Down through the ages, repentance has been watered down to mean "penance, to feel sorry for, contrite." Even Merriam-Webster defines "repent" as "to feel or show you are sorry for something bad or wrong that you did and you want to do what is right." However, in the New Testament, the Greek word used for repentance is *metanoia*, meaning "a change of mind and heart accompanied by regret and a change of conduct." Modern teachings on repentance appear to present it backward: if you show regret and a change of conduct, it will change your heart and mind.

Many deliverance and inner healing ministries lead a person through rituals and declarations of repentance. However, simply saying something doesn't make it so. Saying the words, "I repent" doesn't change one's heart and thinking. Neuroscientist Dr. Carolyn Leaf describes research that shows it takes twenty-one days of confronting a thought to stop it, and it takes sixty-six days to change to a new habit or pattern of thinking. Repentance is a process of change.

See the clarity when we put the correct definition in place of the word "repentance" or "repent":

> *Godly sorrow brings repentance* [a change in heart and thinking] *that leads to salvation and leaves no regret, but worldly sorrow brings death.*
> 2 Corinthians 7:10 (brackets mine)

> *Repent* [change your heart and thinking] *then, and turn to God so that your sins may be wiped out, that times of refreshing may come from the Lord.*
> Acts 3:19 (brackets mine)

> *...now he commands all people everywhere to repent* [change in heart and thinking].
> Acts 17:30b (brackets mine)

Peter replied, "Repent [change your heart and thinking]
*and be baptized every one of you in the name of Jesus
Christ for the forgiveness of your sins, and you will
receive the Holy Spirit."*
Acts 2:38 (brackets mine)

Change your heart and thinking *from* what *to* what? There
is another kingdom where the laws and principles are different
from the one Jesus preached, and that is the kingdom of darkness.
The kingdom of darkness is simply the realm of the natural, with
our human nature way of thinking under the subtle influence of
the enemy. As humans, we were all born into this dark world.
As followers of Jesus, we are called to focus on changing our
kingdom of darkness, human nature way of thinking to Kingdom
of heaven, or Kingdom of light, thinking.

The message is "there is a new Kingdom." Jesus' presence
on earth brought this new Kingdom, where things are nothing
like the old kingdom. In the old kingdom, there are rules to live
by, laws of nature like gravity and motion. We are also ruled by
our human nature, influenced by the destructive purposes of the
enemy of our souls. Satan's mission is to steal, kill, and destroy.
In John 10:10, Jesus tells us He "came to give life," abundant
life: Kingdom life. In this new Kingdom, everything is different.
You could say the Kingdom of Light is as different from the
kingdom of darkness as day is from night.

...TO THE POOR

Who are the poor? How are they poor? Is it the financially
poor? At least eighty percent of the world's population lives on
less than ten dollars a day. Nearly half of the world, more than
three billion people, live on less than two dollars and fifty cents
a day. Worldwide, 870 million people do not have enough to eat.
One out of four people live without electricity. So there are a lot
of poor people. What about the emotionally poor, relationally
poor, the physically poor? Everyone would agree all humans

are born spiritually poor. As Paul writes, *"For all have sinned and fall short of the glory of God"* (Romans 3:23). Okay, so everyone is poor. So that means Jesus' message in Luke 4:18-19 is for everyone.

These that have turned the world upside down are come hither also.
Acts 17:6, KJV

In Acts, Paul was accused of turning the world upside down. How is the Kingdom of Light upside down from the kingdom of darkness? To be considered "great" in this world, you climb your way up the social, financial, or power structure. Presidents, CEOs, and other leaders are viewed as being powerful and successful. If you want to be great in His Kingdom, you must be the servant of all. The last—the poor—in the natural kingdom will be the first in the Kingdom of heaven. That is why we must change the way we think, because the good news is there is another Kingdom that functions differently than to what we are accustomed!

...HE HATH SENT ME TO HEAL THE BROKENHEARTED

In this Kingdom of the supernatural realm, there is healing for the broken heart, deliverance for the captive, recovery of spiritual sight relationship with the Father, liberty from the bruises, and a calling as favorites of the Father. This good Kingdom news is what I call the path to wholeness, because besides having a place to go after we die, we need wholeness for right now.

*As the prophet Isaiah promised, "His names will be: Amazing Counselor, Strong God, Eternal Father, **Prince of Wholeness**. His ruling authority will grow, and there'll be no limits to the **wholeness** he brings."*
Isaiah 9:6-7, MSG (bold mine)

So who are the brokenhearted? A better question might be, "Who has *not* been brokenhearted?" A broken heart is a sorrowful heart broken by the loss of love. All humans have a deep emotional need to be loved and accepted. When these love needs are not met due to any number of circumstances, there is a deep grieving of the soul. In the core of a person's being one feels unloved, unwanted, rejected, not enough, abandoned. These then become a person's identity.

Brokenhearted people may try to fix their hearts by looking for love in people and things, performance, and prestige. Jesus said He came to heal the brokenhearted, this deep brokenness in the human soul.

...TO PREACH DELIVERANCE TO THE CAPTIVES

Jesus/Yeshua comes from the name "Joshua," which means "deliverance." Jesus came as the Deliverer from the power of sin in natural human behavior, and most of all—as His life demonstrated—as Deliverer from the influences of the evil one.

As Paul writes, *"Opponents must be gently instructed, in the hope that God will grant them repentance leading them to a knowledge of the truth, and that they will come to their senses and escape from the trap of the devil, who has taken them captive to do his will"* (2 Timothy 2:25-26). *"The reason the Son of God appeared was to destroy the devil's work"* (1 John 3:8b). Jesus the Deliverer set captives free by casting out demons.

Everywhere Jesus went, He healed the sick and cast out demons. There are twenty-six accounts in the Gospels of Jesus casting out demons. He also commissioned and empowered his disciples to cast out demons. *"When Jesus had called the Twelve together, he gave them power and authority to drive out all demons and to cure diseases, and he sent them out to proclaim the Kingdom of God and to heal the sick"* (Luke 9:1-2).

Then some time later they saw the results of the power of His name: *"The seventy-two returned with joy and said, 'Lord, even the demons submit to us in your name'"* (Luke 10:17).

Jesus came as the Deliverer to show us how to cast out demons by indeed casting out demons. Before ascending to his Father, Jesus instructed His followers this way: *"These are some of the signs that will accompany believers: They will throw out demons in my name"* (Mark 16:17b, MSG).

In Ephesians 4:27 Paul admonishes: *do not give the devil a foothold.* Imagine a rock climbing wall. A foothold is one of those little bumps that the climber can use to climb up the wall. What Paul is saying is do not give the enemy a place to climb all over you. We are held captive by our sinful thoughts and behaviors. Since the moment we were born, we have given place to the demonic to work in our wounded emotions and wrong beliefs; therefore, we all need deliverance. Jesus gave His believers the authority and the directive to cast out these demons empowered by the Spirit of Christ, just as the disciples did.

...AND RECOVERING OF SIGHT TO THE BLIND

I have heard many sermons that this statement is about physical healing. However, what if one were born blind? The word "recovering" suggests one once had something. That takes me back to a time when mankind could see God. In Genesis 3, we are told God would walk and talk with Adam and Eve in the cool of the day. Adam and Eve had a face-to-face, spiritual sight relationship with their Creator and then lost it. Since that day, all of mankind has been born spiritually blind, without a relationship with our Creator. Jesus came to restore the intimacy of that relationship, and restore the ability to "see" into the realm of the Kingdom, to walk with Him, to talk with Him, and to sense God's presence.

...TO SET AT LIBERTY THEM THAT ARE BRUISED

This appears to be a peculiar statement at first glance. You would think a bruise would require healing. However, consider a look at the deep bruises of your life. These wounds come from the hurtful words and actions of others. "Can't you do anything right?" "You're exactly like your mother, or father, or great uncle Bob." "You were supposed to be born a boy instead of a girl." Sometimes it's the rejection, abandonment, or neglect, as well as the physical, mental, emotional, and sexual abuse that tell you that you are not a valued human being. You're a worthless object. Whatever the words or actions, we use them all to create a perception of our identity, our value, or lack thereof.

The old saying, "Sticks and stones will break my bones but words will never hurt me" is not true. Emotional bruises go deep and bring destruction to the core of a person's being. These wounds come from the hurtful words and actions of others. Just as a severe bruise to the body hinders each movement with pain, the deep bruises of life rule our every thought, belief, and behavior like a cruel taskmaster.

Why "liberty" and not "freedom?" Modern dictionaries define "liberty" and "freedom" interchangeably. Is there a difference? A word-study from older dictionaries shows there is a difference. "Freedom" is best described as the absence of bondage. "Liberty" is the ability to *think* free.

Consider the trained horses you see on TV or in Western movies. The cowboy rides up, jumps off his horse, and runs off on foot, chasing the outlaws. What does his horse do? It stands, untethered. Why? Ever since it was young it was haltered with a rope tied tightly to a weight or hook in the ground. Unable to move freely, it learned when the reins or lead rope are hanging to the ground, "I am bound and unable to move."

So is the horse free? It is not actually tied up; the horse is technically free. Does the horse have liberty? No. He is not able to think freely because of his training, his experience, and the perception of bondage that he learned years ago.

We need *liberty* from the bruises that rule us.

...TO PREACH THE ACCEPTABLE YEAR OF THE LORD.

This statement is a reference to the Year of Jubilee. In Leviticus, the Year of Jubilee was to be a year of rest. Every 50th year, the Hebrew children were to rest from work, planting, and harvest. It was to be a year of celebration of the Lord's favor and provision. The harvest years prior to Jubilee had to be abundant in order to last through the 50th year celebrations and also the year following when planting began again.

Jesus' arrival was a declaration of the Lord's favor. He came as a fulfillment of the Old Covenant with the children of Israel, and to establish the New Covenant with both the Jews and the Gentiles as favored in Christ. As Paul told us, *"There is neither Jew nor Gentile, neither slave nor free, nor is there male and female, for you are all one in Christ Jesus"* (Galatians 3:28, NLT).

Because of our blindness, bruises, and brokenness, it is difficult to grasp the concept of "favor," let alone what it means to have favor with God. Most Christians have been taught to fear the judgment of God, the anger of God, and the disappointment of God. We do not live as if we're already under His favor as children of the Most High and joint heirs with Jesus.

Jesus' life demonstrated Kingdom living. He declared provision for people's needs whether it was food, wine, healing, deliverance, calming a storm, or raising a dead friend back to life. Many times Jesus proclaimed the Kingdom is here, the Kingdom is near, and the Kingdom is upon you. We have yet to grasp the depth of what Jesus tried to convey about the Kingdom.

What we do know is that Jesus came to heal broken hearts, deliver us from demonic infestation, and give liberty from the bruises that rule us. He came to bring us into intimate relationship with the Father and Creator just as when He walked this earth.

Chapter 5

THE SOUL IN DARKNESS

After several years of giving Deliverance Conferences and teaching on Prophetic Deliverance with Tim, I started to share the healing journey that needs to take place after deliverance. To understand what inner healing is and why we need soul-healing, it is important to see how we were broken in the first place, and what this damage does to the human soul.

SPIRIT, SOUL AND BODY

We humans are three parts. Paul mentioned these three parts in 1 Thessalonians 5:23, *"May your whole spirit, soul and body."* We are spirit, the part that was breathed into mankind and interacted with The Creator. When Adam and Eve disobeyed, they no longer saw themselves through Father's eyes, but saw themselves through their shame and guilt. Mankind from that point on was born spiritually dead. Paul writes, *"And you he made alive, who were dead in trespasses and sins"* (Ephesians 2:1, NKJV).

When we accept Christ as our Savior, we are born anew into the Kingdom of God. There is a spiritual birth: *"And in Christ your spirit is alive"* (Romans 8:10). We come alive in Christ: *"But because of his great love for us, God, who is rich in mercy, made us alive with Christ even when we were dead in transgressions—it is by grace you have been saved"* (Ephesians 2:4-5).

Humans are also physical bodies. Regrettably our physical body ages, decays, and eventually dies. When we accept Christ as Savior, we may live in the blessings of physical health and healing of the body, but our bodies do not change to "spiritual bodies." That happens when we see Jesus face to face: *"But we know that when Christ appears, we shall be like him, for we shall see him as he is"* (1 John 3:2b).

Also, we are living souls: *"And the LORD God formed man of the dust of the ground, and breathed into his nostrils the breath of life; and man became a living soul"* (Genesis 2:7, KJV). The term spirit and soul are used interchangeably in scripture: *"The human spirit can endure in sickness, but a crushed spirit who can bear?"* (Proverbs 18:14). The soul is described as the spirit of a person, a person's identity. This spirit/soul consists of the mind, the will, and emotions. These three are tightly interwoven as biological functions that make for the identity of the individual. However, unlike movement and actions, they are unseen.

The mind is how a person thinks. Through human intellect and reasoning we form beliefs. The will is what we believe and therefore desire. The emotions are what we feel, in connection to what we think and believe.

At salvation our souls are born anew. We have the choice to submit to a renewal process. Paul describes this process in Romans 12:1-2:

> *Therefore, I urge you, brothers and sisters, in view of God's mercy, to offer your bodies as a living sacrifice, holy and pleasing to God—this is your true and proper worship. Do not conform to the pattern of this world, but be transformed by the renewing of your mind. Then*

you will be able to test and approve what God's will
is—his good, pleasing and perfect will.

This poses another question: What is God's will?

GOD'S WILL

We all have heard and you may have also questioned, "What is God's will for my life?" When a person is talking about God's will, one is usually asking, "What does God want me to *do*?" So what is God's *will*? According to Romans 12:1-2, His good, pleasing, and perfect will is that we be transformed by the renewing of our minds. Transformed from what to what? I believe Paul is talking about a transformation from our innate human tendencies to a Kingdom perspective that Jesus demonstrated in His life on earth. Paul experienced such a transformation through divine revelations from the ascended Christ.

God is not as interested in what we *do*, but rather in what we *are*, or *become*, conformed to the image of his Son. The question we should ask is not, "What would Jesus do?" but rather, "Who is Jesus in us?"

As Paul declares in Romans 8:29, *"For those God foreknew he also predestined to be conformed to the image of his Son, that he might be the firstborn among many brothers and sisters."*

KINGDOM OF DARKNESS THINKING

Unfortunately, from the moment we are born, we come into this life with a kingdom of darkness thinking and mentality. Paul explains it in Ephesians 2:1-3 like this:

As for you, you were dead in your transgressions and
sins, in which you used to live when you followed the
ways of this world and of the ruler of the kingdom of

the air, the spirit who is now at work in those who are disobedient. All of us also lived among them at one time, gratifying the cravings of our sinful nature and following its desires and thoughts. Like the rest, we were by nature objects of wrath.

Kingdom of darkness thinking is simply the operation of our fallen human nature under the influence of the enemy. Luke describes how we have a victim mentality and are ruled by the anxieties of life: *"Be careful, or your hearts will be weighed down with carousing, drunkenness, and the anxieties of life, and that day will close on you suddenly like a trap"* (Luke 21:34). *"An unbelieving heart is turned away from God,"* a writer shows us in Hebrews 3:12. The ruler of the kingdom of darkness has purposed our destruction and uses our moral downfall for his purposes to steal, kill, and destroy (John 10:10).

Also, when we accept Christ as Savior and decide to live for Him, we don't automatically leave our kingdom of darkness thinking. We begin our new life by a change in belief. We recognize our need for a savior and salvation but we also bring our kingdom of darkness, human nature, and a lot of unbelief with us as we enter the Kingdom of Light.

THE HOUSE OF SOUL

Let's picture the soul as a house with many rooms. We humans, of course, are more complex and not as compartmentalized as a building. I like to use a house to demonstrate the workings of our souls that houses our minds (what we think), our wills (what we believe), and our emotions (what we feel). This makes it easier to see how our soul is the repository of our broken identity.

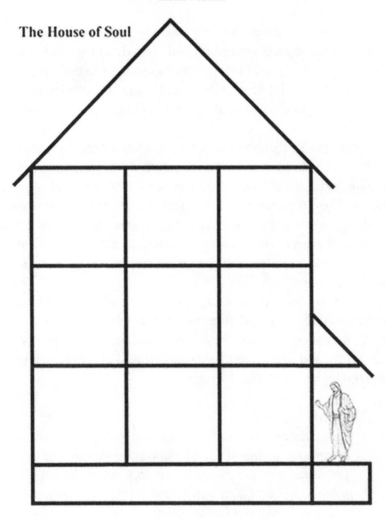

The House of Soul

IDENTITY IS THE FOUNDATION

The foundation of this house bears the weight of the soul's identity. From the moment of conception, the human soul gathers information from many sources to build an identity and define one's existence.

Because we are of Adam's race, we inherit shame, guilt, fear, condemnation, rejection, and hatred, along with many other human tendencies that are used as sources to build identity. There are also influences of the Enemy who, as he did with Eve, speaks subtle lies, causing us to doubt God and believe God has rejected us.

There is also the influence of our human nature. In Galatians 5:16, Paul lists how our human nature acts. The King James Version calls it "the flesh" and then lists an array of strange things: *"Now the works of the flesh are manifest, which are these: adultery, fornication, uncleanness, lasciviousness, idolatry, witchcraft, hatred, variance, emulations, wrath, strife, seditions, heresies, envyings, murders, drunkenness, revelings, and such like"* (Galatians 5:16, KJV).

When we look at this list, we don't relate to it. We may understand adultery and fornication, but what are emulations, strife, seditions, and revelings? No, we don't do idolatry or witchcraft and, my goodness, never murder. That is why I appreciate the list in *The Message*:

> *It is obvious what kind of life develops out of trying*
> *to get your own way all the time: repetitive, loveless,*
> *cheap sex; a stinking accumulation of mental and*
> *emotional garbage; frenzied and joyless grabs for*
> *happiness; trinket gods; magic-show religion; paranoid*
> *loneliness; cutthroat competition; all-consuming-yet-*
> *never-satisfied wants; a brutal temper; an impotence*
> *to love or be loved; divided homes and divided lives;*
> *small-minded and lopsided pursuits; the vicious habit of*
> *depersonalizing everyone into a rival; uncontrolled and*
> *uncontrollable addictions; ugly parodies of community.*
> *I could go on.*
> Galatians 5:16, MSG

Every human being has an insatiable emotional need for unconditional love and acceptance. Human nature is focused on these unmet needs. Listed above are some of the behaviors that are the result of that focus and the human drive to meet those needs. A later chapter will further discuss how our behavior is actually the fruit of what is at the root.

The family is another powerful influence on identity. As they develop, children are easily afflicted with a distorted sense of identity. Much of what we believe about ourselves is firmly rooted in us before the age of nine, in our impressionable years.

Who, then, does not have an accumulation of mental and emotional garbage as Galatians 5 lists? That is what fills the rooms of our souls. Ever see the TV show *Hoarders*? It portrays the lives of people who suffer from a psychological disorder called "disposophobia," which is the fear of throwing away, or compulsive hoarding. That is what the houses of our souls look like. Each room, each square inch packed full of all the experiences, pain, memories, beliefs, and emotions of our lives that are all tainted by our kingdom of darkness experiences.

Fill in the rooms of the diagram of the house with your own personal mental and emotional garbage. I wrote "control" in the center room of my house because of my history with my personal issues. You don't have to be demonized with a control spirit to have control issues. People use control as a way to try to manage uncontrollable lives and avoid the pain and fear of being controlled by others.

We can write in a room the experiences of offense and abuse. Include painful emotions of fear, anger, anxiety, rejection, hatred, shame, and condemnation. The rooms fill up and our souls look like the cartoon junk closet waiting to burst open with the slightest touch. Like the junk drawers, closets, and storage rooms in our physical homes, our souls are filled with our mental and emotional "stuff" simply because we don't know what to do with all the pain.

In an attempt to survive the traumas of life, we fill more rooms with our coping behaviors of control, codependency, obsessions, and addictions. From the moment we are born, our souls are filled with beliefs influenced by the kingdom of darkness, so our human nature is driven to fill our unmet needs.

WHO LIVES IN THE DARKNESS?

The enemy is an opportunist; therefore, Paul warns us: *"Be alert and of sober mind. Your enemy the devil prowls around like a roaring lion looking for someone to devour"* (1 Peter 5:8). He sees all this darkness in us and recognizes it as an opportunity for his purposes: to steal, kill, and destroy. As Paul said in Ephesians 4:27, we have given the enemy a foothold, a place of access. If he can't keep us from coming to Christ, he will at least continue to assist our ineffectiveness in Christ's Kingdom. This describes the work of demonization.

As it says in 2 Peter 2:4, *"For if God did not spare angels when they sinned, but sent them to hell, putting them in chains of darkness to be held for judgment."* Demons are confined to darkness; not where there is an absence of physical light, but where there is an absence of Jesus, the light of the world, and the Kingdom of Light, God's truth and revelation. Our souls are full of darkness thoughts and beliefs that are more in agreement with the accuser of the believer than with the giver of life abundant.

Chapter 6

SALVATION TO THE SOUL

If you declare with your mouth, "Jesus is Lord," and
believe in your heart that God raised him from the
dead, you will be saved. For it is with your heart that
you believe and are justified, and it is with your mouth
that you profess your faith and are saved.
Romans 10:9-10

Let's say this house of the soul represents the life of most
people who call themselves Christians. At some point they
invite Jesus Christ into their lives. As it says in Romans 10:9-10,
we confess Jesus is Lord and believe God raised Him from the
dead. John writes, *"Yet to all who did receive him, to those who*
believed in his name, he gave the right to become children of
God" (John 1:12). We accept the invitation to receive Christ and
believe in Him, but we come with all our physical, emotional,
intellectual, and spiritual baggage. We desperately want to live
for Jesus Christ and want Him to be the "Lord" of our lives,
but like most who call themselves Christians, we struggle with
the Christian walk because we attempt only to add Jesus to our
lives. We try to make some changes in behaviors that we think
are required for "converts," such as going to church, reading the
Bible, praying, and doing good deeds. However, for the most

part, much of the mental and emotional baggage still remains in the rooms of our house of soul.

We essentially allow Jesus to paint the outside of our house and do some landscaping. What about the inside? Well, Jesus called the Pharisees "whitewashed tombs," all pretty on the outside but stinking of death on the inside. He knew what was in their hearts, their accumulation of mental and emotional baggage, their *darkness* thinking.

I find it interesting that in Revelation 3:20 Jesus says to the Laodicean church, *"Here I am! I stand at the door and knock. If anyone hears my voice and opens the door, I will come in and eat with him, and he with me."* Even though we often hear this scripture as a salvation plea to the lost soul, Jesus is actually making this plea to believers! Why? Because we've only added Jesus to our lives and have left Him standing on the porch of our house of soul.

In the homes we live in, we have rooms and closets we don't let anyone see. There, we hide our stuff. Like Adam and Eve, we hide from Him, afraid to let our Creator see what we've accumulated. Oh, we may have a living room or foyer that we allow guests into, but we don't allow them to go wandering throughout our house to see what is in the basement or attic. Actually, *we* don't even know what is there. We spend our lives ignoring what is stashed away simply because it is so painful to remember. Besides, we don't know what to do with the pain.

Let's look again at Jesus' invitation, *"Here I am! I stand at the door and knock. If anyone hears my voice and opens the door, I will come in and eat with that person, and they with me"* (Revelation 3:20, KJV).

What is most overlooked in Revelation 3:20 is the last line: *"I will come in and eat with that person and they with me."* Jesus is making a reference to an ancient eastern custom of hospitality, *koinonia*. We know *koinonia* is Greek for "fellowship," but there is a much richer, deeper meaning. It was once explained to us by a visitor from a Middle Eastern country in this word picture.

She described that in ancient days, as well as in some countries today, a meal consisted of a big pot of broth with some morsels of vegetables or meat. There were no individual bowls or spoons used, but each person had a hunk of bread that they would form into a grabber. Each would dip his bread into the pot, soak up some broth then take a bite. This would be repeated over and over by each person at the meal.

Today we would call this double dipping, a social *faux pas* resulting in passing germs to others. *Koinonia*, as Jesus describes, is the act of literally becoming a part of one another. As we each put ourselves into the pot, we are also taking in a part of each other. Jesus is saying if you will open the door, I will become a part of you and you will become a part of me. That also sounds like His prayer, *"that all of them may be one, Father, just as you are in me and I am in you. May they also be in us so that the world may believe that you have sent me"* (John 17:21).

DELIVERANCE LEADS TO INNER HEALING

Now let us consider that this soul, this house, has experienced Prophetic Deliverance. Through the exercise of the gifts of the Holy Spirit, and the confirmation by the agreement of two or three persons present, the functional name of the chief spirit, the "strongman," is identified. Jesus describes in Matthew 12:29 how the "strongman," the highest level of demonic infestation in an individual, needs to be identified, and then the strongman with his whole entourage can be cast out. Deliverance evicts the demon "squatters" but the accumulation of mental and emotional baggage still remains. The house of soul still needs a house cleaning. That is the work of inner healing.

Jesus teaches, *"When an impure spirit comes out of a person, it goes through arid places seeking rest and does not find it. Then it says, 'I will return to the house I left'"* (Luke 11:24-16).

When an evil spirit leaves a person, at some point in time it will come back looking for an empty place to inhabit. However, the real danger is it will also bring others. The house needs to have Jesus doing what He said in Luke 4:18: the Holy Spirit must inhabit the rooms that once gave place to the work of the enemy. Inner Healing is you and Jesus opening the rooms of the soul and doing some house cleaning. This means the mental and emotional accumulation needs to be identified and some decisions need to be made about what you're hoarding in your soul.

Even though the term "inner healing" is not found in scripture, there are many scriptures that describe this work of healing the wounds of the soul. In Galatians 2:20 Paul asserts, "I have been crucified with Christ and I no longer live, but Christ lives in me." He has put to death the kingdom of darkness thinking. In Ephesians 4:23 he says we are to be *"made new in the attitude of the mind."* Of course, Romans 12:2b refers to our being *"transformed by the renewing of the mind."*

It has often been taught that renewing the mind is done through attending church or Bible studies more often and praying more. However, Jesus confronted the Pharisees, telling them that cleaning the outside of the cup is not enough. First, clean the inside of the dish, and the outside will be clean too. Apparently, Jesus saw all their religious behavior was not sufficient to bring about an inner transformed life. If that is true, then why do we think that our performance will be any more effective than that of the Pharisees of Jesus' day?

There is much missing even from the Christian counseling profession. I pursued a Pastoral Counseling degree at Oral Roberts University because I assumed one of the most prestigious Christian charismatic universities could certainly teach me how to verbalize what I had experienced, the supernatural component of healing the wounded soul. I learned from every angle how to counsel Christians and assimilate secular counseling practices into biblical principles, but no one ever taught about the supernatural or the power of the Holy Spirit to heal soul wounds.

What happens when we allow Jesus into these rooms and

the Holy Spirit does some supernatural house cleaning? Instead of housing a stinking accumulation of mental and emotional garbage, or as in the Pharisees' case, the stench of death, Galatians 5:22-23a describes what the fruit of our lives can be. The fruit of *His* Spirit is love, joy, peace, forbearance, kindness, goodness, faithfulness, gentleness, and self-control.

Most Christians are trying to "perform fruit," thinking this is how they are supposed to act. Yet, their fruit is growing in the toxic soul of their stinking accumulation of mental and emotional garbage. If you try to grow fruit in toxic soil, you get toxic fruit. What is toxic love? It is love with an agenda—conditional, self-serving codependency. How about toxic kindness? It is being nice, which is counterfeit, also having a selfish agenda. Joy is a mask and peace is fleeting. Since the beginning of creation, everything reproduces after its own kind. Whatever is at the root is produced in its fruit.

THE PURPOSE OF WHOLENESS AND INNER HEALING

Inner healing is the means to pursue wholeness. Inner healing is what Jesus presented in Luke 4:18. Besides healing the broken heart and providing liberty from the bruises that rule us, this starts with deliverance from the demons infesting the wounded soul.

Wholeness is where He wants to take us.

Ephesians 4:13, as translated in *The Message*, describes the purpose of the Inner Healing journey toward wholeness:

> *To train Christ's followers in skilled servant work,*
> *working within Christ's body, the church, until we're*
> *all moving rhythmically and easily with each other,*
> *efficient and graceful in response to God's son, fully*
> *mature adults, fully developed within and without, fully*
> *alive like Christ. No prolonged infancies among us,*
> *please. We'll not tolerate babes in the woods, small*

> *children who are an easy mark for impostors. God*
> *wants us to grow up, to know the whole truth and tell*
> *it in love—like Christ in everything. We take our lead*
> *from Christ, who is the source of everything we do. He*
> *keeps us in step with each other. His breath and blood*
> *flow through us, nourishing us so that we will grow up*
> *healthy in God, robust in love.*

The purpose, then, of the work of inner healing and the pursuit of wholeness is to move us from being ruled by kingdom of darkness thinking to Kingdom of Light belief. It is to grow us from spiritual infancy to maturity. We cannot be spiritually mature while remaining emotionally immature, frozen in childhood emotions and beliefs. Inner healing and wholeness help us find God's will for our lives by leaving behind our identity as defined by human nature and finding our true identity as Jesus knew it to be—that we may be one, as He and His Father are one (John 17:22b).

SECTION 3

APPLICATION

Chapter 7

CORE BELIEFS

CORE BELIEFS ARE THE SEED

Sometime after my deliverance, as I pursued His healing, the Lord showed me where a spirit of suicide had entered my life. He took me back to a situation in my childhood when I was about ten or eleven years old. I found myself listening in on my parents, who were having an argument. They always fought, which created a lot of tension in the house when they were both there. I was hiding up the stairs, out of sight, when I heard one of my parents exclaim, "Our marriage was a mistake! We never should have gotten married!" All of a sudden, in the midst of this memory, I could clearly recall thinking, "I'm the oldest child. I must be a mistake,"

In *The Search for Reality*, author Robert McGee writes:

What we are taught, primarily from our parents, becomes a system of beliefs upon which we evaluate all incoming information. It's the grid through which we process our perception of truth and falsehood. Based upon what we witness and experience, coupled with what we are taught, we develop core beliefs that change little throughout life. They are foundational and become our emotional strongholds.

Through the exposure of my core belief—I must be a mistake—my life patterns suddenly became clear. I realized how my life and body were scarred by many types of self-harming, self-punishing behaviors. At twelve I had attempted suicide. Any time I failed at relationships, I would physically punish myself by hitting walls with my fists or head. My promiscuity was an attempt at trying to find attention at the cost of my purity. Even after giving my life to Jesus, I struggled with anorexia and an addiction to exercise to strictly discipline myself.

On the other side of the ditch were my workaholic behaviors through which I attempted to disprove that I was a mistake. As a young wife with three small children, I had my own military sewing business while Tim was in the Air Force. My work was so much in demand that I would sew for ten to twelve hours a day and sometimes around the clock. I reveled in being the "Savior of the Base" as I daily heard the praises of my customers. When I began to hallucinate with my body weight hovering at around one hundred pounds, Tim recognized that I was suffering from burnout, and I agreed to take a one-month sabbatical. At the end of that month, I found myself pregnant with our fourth child. I knew better than to harm my unborn baby, so I began eating again.

When Tim took his first pastorate, I was determined to be the best pastor's wife in the denomination, serving right alongside my husband. That first year of ministry, I was diagnosed with an ulcerous condition and was ordered by the doctor to give up running several of the church's ministries to let my body heal while on medication.

The Lord showed me in that traumatic childhood moment, when I heard my parents say their marriage was a mistake, my child's mind came up with a belief that became a foundational belief about me. A "core belief" settled into the foundation of my identity, determining my worth and value as a person, affecting me for the rest of my life. This bruise in my soul, this wound in my psyche, ruled me, proclaiming I was a mistake. Therefore, I played out this statement either by punishing myself for being alive or trying to disprove I was a mistake through performance and productivity.

In reliving this memory I was shown how, in a traumatic wounding event, we humans have a revelation. We come up with a belief in an attempt to make sense of what we experience. We are information gatherers, always trying to make sense of our world in order to figure out who we are. We take in information and form an identity. Sadly, because of our fallen human nature, the negative, hurtful experiences have more impact than the positive experiences.

Once our brains start collecting negative information, a pattern of negative toxic thoughts and beliefs imprints on the neurons in our brains. Dr. Caroline Leaf, author of Who Switched Off My Brain, describes when we start the pattern of negative, toxic thoughts, our brains attract and absorb more negative, toxic thoughts. Toxic thoughts then build memories that are distorted and harmful along with negative emotions that are based in fear. Toxic thoughts with negative emotions create an attitude, a state of mind, that produces behavior.

WOUNDS FEED CORE BELIEFS

We encounter many situations throughout our lives that wound and re-wound us over and over. What happens when you bump a wound over and over? It doesn't heal but also gets bigger and bigger until it is an ugly festering wound. That toxic core belief gets stronger and stronger as situation after situation, and painful experience upon hurtful experience, feed that belief. Of course, when we compare it to what God says about us, intellectually we can see it is a lie. In our core, deep down inside, for us, it is our perceived truth.

Like a computer program, this wound becomes our programming and we perceive everything through the wounds of our lives. This program of our wounds—this core belief—makes it difficult to perceive God's truth about us. We see that truth in the Word of God and can read it and hear the words, but because it does not conform to our original program, we are unable to download it into our core. Therefore it remains in our heads as intellectual information but is never brought into the core of our being because of our conflicting beliefs already in place.

We have heard people speak of head knowledge that needs to move to heart knowledge. Caroline Leaf speaks of the "brain of the heart," synapses in the heart that make it ultra-sensitive to what you think and feel. It has its own independent nervous system, acts like a conscience, and is the real "intelligent force" behind the intuitive thoughts and feelings we experience. The heart is in constant communication with the brain as well as the rest of the body through biochemical communication systems. The heart has significant influence on the function of the brain and the body. The connections between the heart and the brain check the accuracy and integrity of our thought life. No wonder Jesus declared in Luke 4:18 that He came to "heal the brokenhearted." Our hearts need healing in order to receive Kingdom Truth.

Even though ancient Hebrew culture considers and writes about the heart as the core of a person, the issues of the heart are only a part of our "core." When we pray the Wounded Spirit Prayer, we pray cleansing by the blood of Jesus and healing by the oil of the Holy Spirit over three parts: the head and the functions of the brain; the heart, which influences the brain functions; and also the stomach, representing the core, or innermost part of a person.

Have you heard the phrase, "gut reaction"? If you search the Internet, you will find much research being done in the area of the enteric nervous system, otherwise known as the "brain of the gut." "It does much more than merely handle digestion or inflict the occasional nervous pang. The little brain in our innards, in connection with the big one in our skulls, partly determines our mental state and plays key roles in certain diseases throughout the body (Hadhazy)."

That revelation, that gut reaction, that core belief, therefore determines one's mental state and health. Jesus declared in Luke 4:18 that He came to bring liberty to the bruised because our deep emotional bruises rule us. Yours rule you.

CELLULAR MEMORY

I recently came upon a report about the discovery of "cellular memory." It had been previously understood that memory was stored in the brain. However, situations with organ transplant recipients are challenging old paradigms. Some recipients have experienced the memories of the donors. In one such case, authorities were able to solve a donor's murder and make an arrest.

You may be asking why I am suddenly talking about cellular memory. I found this information fascinating as biological proof of wounds and bruises that rule us.

In *The Healing Code*, Dr. Alexander Lloyd describes how we have information implanted in our memory. All of our life experiences are stored in our memory. The brains in our head, in our heart, and in our gut collect this information and send it out to be stored in every cell of our bodies. That is how our memory can be activated by any of our senses—touch, taste, smell, hearing, and sight. We mostly think of a memory as recalling a picture in our minds, but memory can be recalled through any of the senses with no picture.

Of our stored memory, only ten percent is termed conscious memory. That means we can only recall ten percent of what is in our memory. The other ninety percent of our memory is subconscious or unconscious memory, which is either difficult to retrieve or irretrievable altogether. Buried deep in the unconscious are not only the facts, figures, and pictures of our life events, but also the distorted perceptions and meanings we put to ourselves in those events, as in my "I'm a mistake" story.

The problem with this information is that without our

realizing it on a conscious level, it works like a type of "security system" to all other incoming information. As in our homes, a security system keeps out whatever does not comply with the standard that has been set—the standard set by our core belief.

To demonstrate this, let's pick a core belief that says, "I am unworthy of love." No matter how hard we try in our conscious mind to believe and receive God's truth from His Word that says God loves us, when met with the unconscious core belief, guess which one wins? Our core belief wins, and conflicting information is rejected. Does this mean God's Word has no power? Absolutely not! This shows God does not violate our will, which is what we believe. Our core beliefs decide what information will be received or rejected.

This process has been proved through Dr. Lloyd's medical research by using a stress test to measure the biological response to the power of a core belief. When the person tested spoke a conflicting statement to his core belief, like "I am worthy of love," his body recorded stress. When he spoke his core belief statement, "I am unworthy of love," there was no show of stress in his vital signs.

So the question is this: how do we expose this core belief and implant God's truth? Stay tuned. We will get there, but first let's talk about strongholds.

STRONGHOLDS

Throughout our lives we build a pattern of belief about our identity, thought by thought. Psychology calls these patterns a schema of thought. 2 Corinthians 10:4-5 calls it a stronghold. We have many "strongholds" (or patterns of thinking and beliefs about life) about others, as well as about ourselves. Patterns of thought include our talents and abilities. We can have a stronghold of thinking about music, sports, or literature. We have a stronghold of belief about ourselves, our identity, and our worth and value as a person.

Because of the painful life experiences and the negative

beliefs we carry, we develop our identity as a stronghold of worthlessness, thought by thought, brick by brick. "I'm a mistake. Nobody loves me. I am a failure, unwanted, rejected, worthless." These core beliefs lay the foundation of the walled fortress we hide behind and call our identity. When we feel threatened, we hide behind its walls and attempt to comfort ourselves with thoughts of self-pity: "Oh woe is me, nobody cares. After all, I am alone because I am not wanted or valued."

When we create a fortress made of these types of thoughts, we have a place of darkness in our souls, a moral darkness that does not allow in the One who is Light. Jude 1:6 says, *"And the angels who did not keep their positions of authority but abandoned their proper dwelling—these he has kept in darkness, bound with everlasting chains for judgment on the great day."*

Because of this darkness thinking in us, we give place to the enemy to steal, kill, and destroy. That is what demonization is. Demons see an opportunity to influence our own dark, toxic, negative beliefs about ourselves. "How right you are," he slyly persuades us. The enemy uses every means of deception to make sure we keep building that stronghold brick by brick.

We have many patterns of thought and belief, and as I said before, not all strongholds are bad or have a negative meaning. However, there is one who wants to be our stronghold, our place of safety. In ancient civilizations, kings and rulers would build fortressed cities to protect the people under their responsibility. It gave them a sense of safety and security from invading enemies. David well describes how *"The name of the Lord is a strong tower: the righteous run to it and are safe"* (Proverbs 18:10).

2 Corinthians 10:5b (NKJV) says to *"take captive every thought that sets itself up against the knowledge of God."* This is not about confronting other people in what they believe. This is about confronting our *own* core beliefs that are not in agreement with God's Word. Later on, I will share some practical information on how to "take our thoughts captive" and make them obedient and submissive to God's Word and truth.

Judgments

Finally, let's take a look at how our core beliefs are negative judgments we make about ourselves. Remember my "I'm a mistake" story? Nobody told me that I was a mistake. I came up with that by myself.

In *How to Stop the Pain*, James Richards describes, "nothing has the power to hurt us until we give it significance." We give significance to what people say and do. We use their words and actions to make a judgment—a negative judgment—about ourselves.

In Matthew 7:1, Jesus says, *"Do not judge, or you too will be judged."* We think that means God will judge us, but there is no more condemnation for those who are in Christ Jesus (Romans 8:1). Jesus goes on to say in verse 2, *"For in the same way you judge others, you will be judged, and with the measure you use, it will be measured to you."* Not only will you be judged *by others* with the measure you use, but you will also judge *yourself* with that same measure.

For example, if I judge that a person is treating me like I'm stupid, first of all I have judged the intention of the person. I have assumed what they are thinking and the motivation behind his or her action. Second, I then judge myself: "Ah, therefore I am stupid!"

Voila, a core belief!

A core belief is always a negative judgment made about oneself, based upon a situation or experience with another person. It is always in the form of a short, "I am," statement. Core beliefs are the glasses we look through that influence our perception of everything: our perception of God, our perception of relationships with others, and our sense of our own identity. What we *perceive* is what we *receive*, and it therefore becomes what we *believe*.

Core beliefs are why life's wounds are so painful.

Core beliefs are why the bruises rule us.

The healing all of us need is from our own negative self-judgments, our core beliefs.

Chapter 8

EXPOSING THE ROOTS

GROWING WHAT IS PLANTED

If you want to grow beans, you have to plant bean seeds. If your garden is growing okra, you must have planted okra, not beans. Everything reproduces after its own kind. Apple trees grow apples and peach trees grow peaches. It's as simple as that.

Is your life producing fear, anxiety, and anger? What if your life is filled with broken relationships, unfilled potential, and loss of purpose? Look to the roots. There is something deeply planted and growing that fruit.

In trying to understand life's fruit, let's look at this progression of growth from a seed to a plant. Deep below the surface—in the core of your being—stored in the ninety percent of unconscious memory is the memory of a painful, emotionally wounding situation. Perhaps there have been several situations throughout your life that have severely impacted you and wounded you to the core of your being.

Situation

In the midst of that painful situation, there was a negative revelation. In an attempt to make sense of the experience we asked ourselves, "What does this say about me?" It is our human nature to gather information as we attempt to understand our experience and find out who we are. Therefore a judgment was made. (As I said in a previous chapter, it is also our human nature to gather negative information about ourselves because of the shame factor.) A core belief was birthed. When compared to what God says in His Word, we should have seen that it is a lie. To us, it was our perceived truth. Remember, what we perceive is what we believe. So from that time on, a belief in a lie has lived in that wound.

Faulty thinking patterns then sprout from the wound. These patterns feed the need for performance in order to help us undo or deny the core belief along with patterns of punishment that agree with and reinforce it.

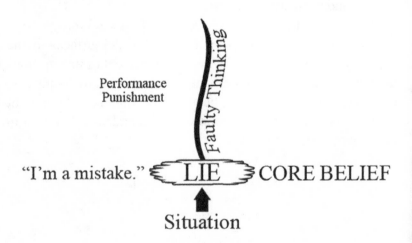

Closer to the surface are our painful emotions of anger, fear, anxiety, rejection, insecurity, worthlessness, or depression. We try to keep them hidden below the surface, but when pressure comes, or if we start digging, the emotional pain is what surfaces first. Often this emotional pain keeps people from going deeper to expose the roots, the true source of the pain.

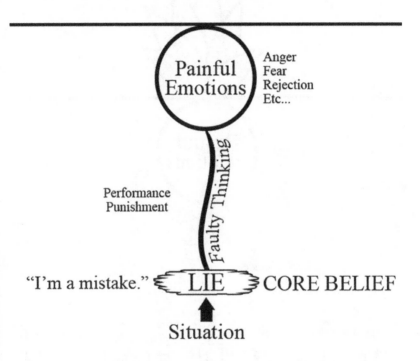

Above the surface, where everyone can see, is our Problem Behaviors.

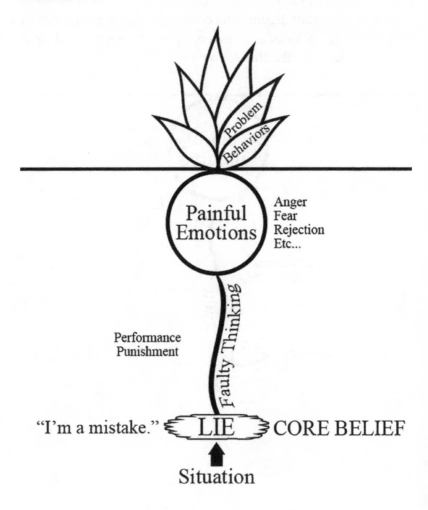

Our Problem Behaviors easily show up within the pressure of relationships. When Jesus was asked, "What is the greatest commandment?" He replied, "Love the Lord your God with all your heart and with all your soul and with all your mind." This is the first and greatest commandment. And the second is like it: "Love your neighbor as yourself" (Matthew 22:37-39). Jesus said the greatest commandments are about relationship with God, relationship with others, and relationship with yourself. That last relationship is probably the most difficult. Throughout Christianity, we are taught to hate ourselves. Paul tells us to put to death the human nature, but we are never told to despise ourselves. It's the opposite; we are told to love what God loves.

A good definition of sin, then, is any breach in relationship. Why are relationships so difficult? Because we are ruled in our relationships by what is at the root—our core belief, our negative judgment about ourselves.

Let's say again a person's core belief is "I am unworthy of love." Then how can that person function in relationships? This core belief doesn't allow a person to receive love. All humans have a deep emotional need for unconditional love and acceptance. This belief rules them from a bruise deep in their core and sabotages the possibility of a healthy relationship.

It's in our human nature to develop and depend on coping behaviors. Our problem behaviors are the coping behaviors we use to try to *protect* ourselves from being hurt again, to *comfort* the pain deep in the core of our being, and to *fix* our brokenness ourselves.

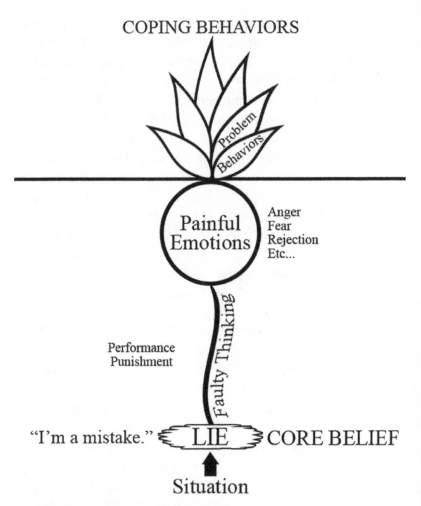

All coping behaviors fall into these three categories: ways we try to protect, comfort, and fix ourselves.

PROTECT OURSELVES

We try desperately to protect ourselves from getting hurt again. We learn early in life that it is dangerous to trust people because people let us down. Also, because we are deeply wounded, we attempt to control others in order to avoid pain and protect the wounds we already carry. Withdrawal and isolation are ways people try to protect themselves from hurts in relationships. I feel the most-used protective coping behavior is denial. We deny we are wounded. We deny we get hurt in relationships. We deny we want or need relationships. We deny we are the source of relationship issues. Denial is a strong coping behavior. To many people, denial is a lying friend.

COMFORT OURSELVES

It appears that our national motto is "Life, liberty, and the avoidance of pain at all costs!" Billions of dollars are spent on the "drug of choice" to stop the pain deep in the soul, whether it be drugs, alcohol, sex, money, or codependent and dysfunctional relationships. Even Christians have their "drugs." How about food, TV, shopping, and the accumulation of possessions? As a musician in worship bands for years, I have seen Christians "addicted" to charismatic worship and the physical adrenaline "high" it produces. What about our Christian performance? We have all heard over and over again from the pulpit that all we need to do is pray more, read our Bibles more, and go to church more.

The cycle of addiction exists because whatever is used to subdue pain has only a temporary effect. Eventually the pain returns and with more intensity. Therefore a greater painkiller is sought, and thus the cycle of addiction continues.

FIX OURSELVES

Look at all the ways we humans are trying to make ourselves better. We think, "If I could change I will feel loved and accepted." So we use diet, exercise, makeup, surgery, life coaches, and success programs. Now don't get me wrong. I'm not saying there is anything wrong with trying to change for the better. When we use change to try and fix the brokenness deep within, it is a useless endeavor. What we don't realize is we can't fix what is broken inside, even when we are attempting to fix ourselves through our religious performance.

BEHAVIOR MODIFICATION IS TEMPORARY

Christians are the biggest fixers. We are told in church to stop doing the wrong things and do the right things. We are told going to church more, reading our Bibles more, and praying more will affect change. What we are being taught in church, in Christian counseling, and in spiritual growth self-help books is nothing more than behavior modification, not transformation. Behavior modification is only a temporary means of changing behavior.

While at Oral Roberts University (ORU), one of my professors made the statement, "You have to teach people to do the right thing and then they will be the right thing."

What? I lit up like a Christmas tree! I recall my response in a homework essay and wrote with such energy and determination, "Noooooo! Jesus told the Pharisees you have to clean the inside of the cup first, then the outside will be clean too!" Transformation takes place from the inside out. Please pardon the intensity of passion I have against this point, but what we are being taught in the church is to be good Pharisees!

Pharisees did all the right things. They memorized it all. They prayed. Their lives appeared like the epitome of righteousness in Jesus' day. Yet, Jesus called them "whitewashed tombs." No wonder the Pharisees hated Jesus. He told them that they looked all pretty on the outside but smelled like death and rotting flesh on the inside. Ewww!

What happens when you mow the grass and weeds in your yard? It grows back and sometimes thicker. Why? Because the root system is still in place. Again, secular and Christian behavior modifications are only a temporary means of changing behavior because what is at the root is not changed.

Paul describes transformation in Romans 12:1-2:

Therefore, I urge you, brothers and sisters, in view of God's mercy, to offer your bodies as a living sacrifice, holy and pleasing to God—this is your true and proper worship. Do not conform to the pattern of this world, but be transformed by the renewing of your mind. Then you will be able to test and approve what God's will is—his good, pleasing and perfect will.

Jesus called on us to change the way we think. Paul states we are to be transformed by the renewing of our minds. This is a soul issue, not a behavior issue. If we bring transformation to the soul (what is at the root), then the behavior will change (the top).

All coping behaviors are an attempt at behavior modification. Secular counseling focuses on changing harmful coping behaviors into less harmful and more effective coping behaviors. Here's another look at those coping behaviors. If we are trying to protect ourselves, then we are not allowing Father to protect us. If we are trying to comfort ourselves, then we are not allowing the Holy Spirit to Comfort us. If we are trying to fix our own brokenness, then we are not allowing Jesus to do what He said He came to do in Luke 4:18. We are not letting God be God in our lives. We are trying to be our own god.

JESUS' PLANT

For fun, let's make a Jesus plant. Starting below the root, what is Jesus' original influential situation? Where did He originally come from? What is His source? We see He left His place in glory and was born a baby. I think to leave His glory and to live as a human was a type of traumatic event.

Where we have a *lie* in our wound, Jesus carried with Him *truth*. He functioned in *true thinking*. His emotions were *true emotions* and His behavior was *true behavior*. When His enemies asked about His ministry, Jesus gave them this answer: *"Very truly I tell you, the Son can do nothing by himself; he can do only what he sees his Father doing, because whatever the Father does the Son also does"* (John 5:19b).

Jesus only does what He sees His Father doing and even said, *"I and my Father are one"* (John 10:30). Therefore, Jesus had a true identity based on His source, the Father!

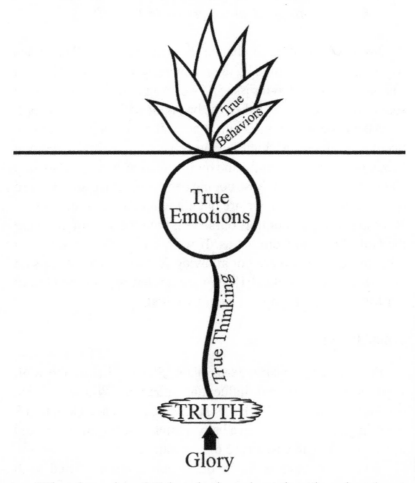

What do *we* have? Take a look again at the other plant (page 78). We have a false identity based on our core belief because we judged ourselves based on what other people said and did.

The healing journey that Jesus presented in Luke 4:18 is to heal us of our false identity and implant in us a true identity based on Him. Jesus said, *"I am the way and the truth and the life"* (John 14:6b). John calls Jesus the Word. Our identity comes from the living Word, our source, our creator.

We know in our minds that God is the source of a Christian's identity, but we do not know it in the core of our being. All our lives, our human nature has fed on another source. Trying to add new information, even good information, from the Word does not change the computer program in our soul. The old program needs to be identified and its power shut down.

I have had well-meaning church folk tell me that their pastor or their Christian friends tell them not to dig into the past stuff. They quote Paul's words in Philippians 3:13b-14: *"Forgetting what is behind and straining toward what is ahead, I press on toward the goal to win the prize for which God has called me heavenward in Christ Jesus."*

What people don't realize is they are defining "forgetting" as Christianized denial. We drag our stuff along behind us like a ball and chain attached to our leg. Hmm. That sounds like religion to me. Actually, our "stuff" is the ball and chain on one leg and our religious performance is the ball and chain on the other leg.

When I used to jog in my recovery years, the route for the charity run was right in front of my house. I got to the place where I could do the short run fairly easily and thought about attempting the longer route. I could hear the Father in my head whisper, "If you want to go the distance, you will have to drop more weight." I knew in the natural that dropping body weight would be better for my knees on a longer distance, but I also knew He didn't mean my body weight.

Forgetting what is behind us means stopping the bruises from ruling us. But how do we do this?

Chapter 9

INTRODUCTION TO
THE FIVE WHOLENESS STEPS

In the previous chapters, I told the story of my healing journey and how was so difficult and disjointed following deliverance. I struggled to understand how to bring healing to the wounds I kept discovering. Like most people, I would focus on the problem behaviors and the painful emotions that needed changing. This kept me in a cycle of performance in an attempt to "act" the way a Christian should. However, my wound was deeper than my behaviors and emotions. Behaviors and emotions are merely the symptoms of the wound in the core, like the plant above the surface.

As I continued to heal, clarity set in. While reading Paul's letters in the New Testament, I started to see a pattern. I combined that with what I learned from my research into inner healing ministries and saw that the wound was in my identity. Tim's message on that fateful Sunday was titled, "Freedom from the Bondage of Shame." Shame was wrapped and twisted around my identity like a cancerous tumor. Shame influenced the first act of Adam and Eve when they hid from their Creator after they disobeyed. Shame has been passed down through the bloodlines of the human race. Shame is why we hide our brokenness, afraid of being culled from the herd and attacked like weak prey. I can't help but wonder if life on earth would be different if, instead of hiding in fear of judgment and punishment, Adam and Eve had run into the Father's arms and confessed what they had done.

They didn't. So our own judgment of shame is what we carry in the wounds of our soul at the core of our being. I have heard so many Christians talk about "the enemy's lies, the devil's lies." Whose lies are they really? They are *ours*. *We* came up with these judgments, these core beliefs. So now that we see they are there, what do we do with them? How do we heal?

The pattern that emerged I now call *The Five Wholeness Steps*. These are five simple steps to guide a person into the Father's healing. They are not magical and should not be used like a ritual. *The Five Wholeness Steps* are a simple tool, used as a pattern of dialog with the Father, Son, and Holy Spirit, guiding the wounded soul into the Healing Presence.

It is interesting to note that after I shared these steps for several years, a paramedic attended one of our retreats. Upon hearing the steps, he commented how they are similar to the protocol used when encountering a wounded person. It would only make sense that the pattern for healing a wound on the body would follow the same pattern for healing a wound in the soul.

Chapter 10

WHOLENESS STEP ONE:
IDENTIFY THE WOUND

*The spirit of a man will sustain his infirmity; but a
wounded spirit who can bear?*
Proverbs 18:14, KJV

The first step appears pretty obvious. If you want a wound to
be treated, you must first identify the wound. As I said before, so
many other teachings have it backward: they attempt to treat the
behaviors and the emotions. They treat the symptoms rather than
the *core belief*, which is the judgment inside the wound.

Ironically, the first step may be the most difficult step because
of what I call the "shame factor." Shame keeps us from exposure.
We fear what being wounded may mean, but fear is belief in a
probability, not in an inevitability. Also, the church has taught us
to ignore the negative and claim the positive. Again, that is plain
"Christianized denial." We fear the judgment of others, which
sadly may be a real possibility, for as it has been said, the church
is an army that shoots its own wounded.

People do things and life happens. You may, perhaps, feel
the pressure as situations squeeze you like a tube of toothpaste.
Whatever is inside is going to come out and usually it is not
pretty. Your response is to try to scoop it all up and stuff it back

in. Instead of blaming your pain on someone else, see it for what it is. It is an opportunity for a wholeness moment, to bring healing to a wound that has been touched.

Often throughout life, wounds are screaming out for healing. Rather than deny the pain or apply more coping behaviors, stop and ask yourself, "What is at the root of this?" After all, as described in the section on cellular memory, your body knows what this core belief is. So does the Holy Spirit. Ask Him to help you identify your negative self-judgment. It will be in the form of an "I am" statement. Remember my "I'm a mistake" story? At the root of your behaviors and emotions is a wound containing a value judgment against your identity.

Religious Christianity has taught us to reject or even rebuke painful emotions or negative thoughts. We should not rebuke the painful emotions of anger or fear. They are not demons; they are the symptoms of your wounded soul. Use them to identify the true source of your pain, the core belief. To uncover your core belief, along with asking the Holy Spirit to show you, ask yourself these types of questions. Then answer with an "I am___" statement:

> "What is my anger/fear saying about me?
> I am _____."

> "What is the negative self-judgment
>   behind this negative thought?
> I am _____."

This first step identifies the wound by identifying the core belief, the negative judgment at the root of the problem behavior, painful emotion, or faulty thinking that may be surfacing. Remember the picture of the plant. You are going for what is at the root.

My *Healing Path Workbook*, the supplement to this text, will coach you with exercises to help you identify your wounds by identifying your core beliefs.

WHOLENESS STEP TWO: CONFESS THE CORE BELIEF

If we confess our sins [our lies; our faulty, negative, toxic, kingdom of darkness thinking], he is faithful and just to forgive us our sins, and to cleanse us from all unrighteousness.
1 John 1:9, KJV (brackets mine)

The next step after identifying a physical wound is to cleanse it of germs and debris, which can lead to infection. If left unchecked, an infection can cause even worse conditions such as blood poisoning, gangrene, loss of limb, or even death.

Cleansing the wound is another step of exposure. 1 John 1:9 mentions a Kingdom process of cleansing: confession.

We recognize in this verse that confession is required for forgiveness. However, what is often overlooked is the cleansing from "unrighteousness" that is offered. Unrighteousness can be defined as sin, or wickedness, but I like to describe unrighteousness as "everything that is not right with us." Our core belief is not right for us. It is negative, toxic, and in agreement with the kingdom of darkness rather than the truth of His kingdom of light.

Many of us have tried for years to rid ourselves of this

negative thinking. We have made positive confessions and quoted scripture until we were blue in the face. Yet, we are only applying the positive confession or scripture to the upper ten percent of our intellectual, conscious level. For others, we bury core beliefs in the deep vault of denial, thinking "out of sight, out of mind." Though we deny their presence, that does not mean their influence has not infiltrated—and therefore toxified—every aspect of our lives.

The purpose of confession is twofold:

You do not delight in sacrifice, or I would bring it;
you do not take pleasure in burnt offerings.
My sacrifice, O God, is a broken spirit; a broken and
contrite heart you, God, will not despise.
Psalm 51:16-17

King David recognized God wants us to surrender our brokenness to Him as a sacrificial offering. Our confession is our surrender, and therefore very important. Instead of the rituals of confession and the lists of sins to confess that are often a part of other deliverance and inner healing ministries' methodology, confession is and should be an intimate conversation between you and God.

Remember the story of the Prodigal Son? When he came to himself, he humbled himself before his father and confessed what he believed: *"The son said to him, 'Father, I have sinned against heaven and against you. I am no longer worthy to be called your son'"* (Luke 15:21). He confessed to his father his false identity, a core belief. Of course, what did the father do? He restored the son's true identity.

Surely, God requires confession of our sin, but we usually make that about our behavior. What God desires is a confession of the sin of false belief about our identity. Our identity is being ruled by the core belief in our wound. We have been warring against this judgment against our identity all our lives, but we are the ones who put it into power and are passively allowing it to rule us. This is the enemy to our identity in the Kingdom. Christians are so obsessed with trying to find their identity in Christ or their purpose in life, when God wants us to surrender the false identity that we have created.

Look at surrender in terms of warfare. In past times, an enemy that was defeated was forced to surrender. That means they had to lay down their weapons and symbols of rule. They were sometimes subjected to a court system where they had to confess to their war crimes and admit their guilt. We are not the defeated ones in this scenario. The bruise that rules us, the core belief, is the enemy that must be surrendered and handed over to the King of the Kingdom.

This step of confession is simply telling God:

"I have sinned against you. I've believed I am _____ (state the core belief). I confess that it is a lie, and I see the evidence in my life and behavior through _____." (You can tell Him the behavioral issues here.)

Another cleansing provision of the Kingdom is the blood of Jesus. Jesus' blood cleanses us of sin: *"But if we are living in the light, as God is in the light, then we have fellowship with each other, and the blood of Jesus, his Son, cleanses us from all sin"* (1 John 1:7).

In the last chapter of Prophet Deliverance, Tim and I share with you the Wounded Spirit Prayer. We pray this prayer, patterned after Jesus' story of the Good Samaritan, after an individual goes through deliverance. It initiates the healing process to the soul. The Good Samaritan poured wine into the man's wounds as antiseptic to cleanse the wounds. Jesus' blood is our cleansing agent. Then the Good Samaritan poured oil into the wounds as a healing salve. The Holy Spirit is our agent of healing, applying the healing balm of Gilead to our wounds. The

Wounded Spirit Prayer can be used in this step to initiate the cleansing of the wounds.

Father, I thank you for your healing presence.
I loose the blood of Jesus for cleansing in the mind, the thinking, and the memories. Bring your cleansing presence in what he (rather than he/she I will just go with he) thinks, believes and stored in the memories. Let the blood of Jesus flow upon the ears, eyes and mouth, these gates where destruction has entered in through what he has heard, seen and spoken. I loose the cleansing blood upon his heart and his emotions, representing the core of his being. Also, I declare the blood cleansing the deep wounds of his inner man, deep into the hidden wounds and secret wounds, and the old wounds.
Now let the oil of the Holy Spirit come. Bring your healing presence upon the mind, thinking, beliefs and memories. Heal the faulty thinking and lies. Heal the pain stored in the memories. Release the oil of healing into the heart and emotions, the broken places. Bring your healing presence into the deep places of the inner man, into the old wounds, the hidden wounds and secret wounds.
Wrap him in your presence like a protective bandage, watching over him and guarding him in this season of healing. Speak your Word of truth and affirmation into his soul, renewing his mind. I release him into your care because you are faithful to heal and restore and renew. And I declare your Kingdom come and your will be done in Jesus name.

Light exposes. The blood cleanses. Confession is exposing it to the light and allowing His blood to cleanse.

Chapter 12

WHOLENESS STEP THREE: HAND IT TO JESUS

*The weapons we fight with are not the weapons of
the world. On the contrary, they have divine power
to demolish strongholds. We demolish arguments
and every pretension that sets itself up against the
knowledge of God, and we take captive every
thought to make it obedient to Christ.*
2 Corinthians 10:4-5

Step three is another step of cleansing the wound. If you
have a wound with a sliver, a shard of glass, or a bullet, the
foreign object needs to be removed.

In the earlier chapters, I described how our thought patterns
are strongholds that we build brick by brick. Throughout our
lives we build a stronghold of belief about our identity. It rules
us in the core of our being. This is the stronghold that needs to
be taken captive and demolished.

I'm sure the verse above is quite familiar to most Christians.
Popular teachers and preachers have told us that we need to
take our thoughts captive. I even heard Dr. Carolyn Leaf on a
television interview talk about this very thing. I was intrigued by
her explanation of how before a thought attaches to the neurons
in our brains, there is a moment in time where we can take

our thoughts captive and disrupt that attachment. I listened for directions on that "taking thoughts captive" process, but there was no further instruction. So let me give you a step-by-step scenario about how to take thoughts/core beliefs captive.

Tim was in the Air Force and served as Security Police. When he went to the police academy, he learned how to apprehend a suspect using this procedure. We have all seen police shows on TV where policemen apprehend suspicious persons. When the police see a suspect running toward them or away from them, what is the first thing they say?

SAY, "STOP!"

On old time police shows, the cops would say, "Stop in the name of the law!"

We say, "Stop in the name of Jesus!" because we have authority in the name of Jesus.

As Paul proclaims, "That at the name of Jesus every knee should bow, in heaven and on earth and under the earth" (Philippians 2:10).

SAY, "I TAKE AUTHORITY OVER _____ (NAME THE CORE BELIEF)."

The next thing the policeman says could be any one of the following: "Assume the position!" "Hands up!" "Against the wall/car!" "Kneel down!" "Spread eagle on the ground!" These are all surrender positions where the policeman is putting himself in a position of authority over the suspect.

Put yourself in a position of authority by declaring your authority. We have authority where we have been given dominion. For us, that includes the domain of our thoughts and beliefs. We need to exercise our authority over our thoughts. It has been described by many as the first place we need to do spiritual warfare. True spiritual warfare is to oust the infestation of demonic squatters by undergoing prophetic deliverance and then take captive the thoughts and beliefs that are against God's Kingdom truth about our identity.

SEARCH AND INTERROGATE

The suspect is in this position of surrender to keep the policeman safe while he is doing the next step, which is searching and interrogating. The policeman is looking for contraband, stuff the suspect should not have, or weapons that may hurt the policeman. At the same time, he is also questioning the suspect: "Who are you?" "Where are you going?" "Why are you here?" "Where do you come from?"

We don't always like to take responsibility for our thoughts and would rather pass if off onto others. We give significance to what other people say and do and use it as a source to define our identity. We make many assumptions about our thoughts and like to blame others or the enemy for the negative, toxic thoughts we think. But as James Richards writes in *How to Stop the Pain*, "nothing has the power to hurt us until we give it significance." As I have previously described about strongholds, demons only use what we give them. A core belief is *our* revelation, *our* judgment about *ourselves*.

I have a non-scientific theory about the sources of our thoughts. While we like to blame the evil one for our bad thoughts, I think only ten percent of our thoughts are from the enemy. Then there is that crowd of Christians who are always going around saying, "God told me this and God told me that." They are tacking God's name on to everything they say in an attempt to give themselves a boost of spirituality as a coping device for their own insecurity. Mostly this practice is used as a means of spiritual abuse, to set oneself above others. I think, generally speaking, only about ten percent of our thoughts come from God.

So that leaves about eighty percent of our thoughts are our own thoughts for which we need to take responsibility. We need to ask ourselves if a thought is in agreement with the biblical, scriptural truth of how God sees us, or if it is more in agreement with how the enemy feels about us.

SAY, "I BIND YOU IN THE NAME OF JESUS!"

In a given situation, all these scenarios may take place quickly; but to be thorough, the policeman always follows a set order. If the policeman finds it necessary, then he or she will handcuff the suspect. We even have a scripture for this step: *"Whatever you bind on earth will be bound in heaven, whatever you loose on earth will be loosed in heaven"* (Matthew 18:18).

SAY, "I RELEASE YOU TO JESUS!"

Once the suspect is handcuffed, he is put into the police car and taken to the police station for further processing. This may entail more questioning that could result in either arrest or release. That is why we train our deliverance teams to use this process in deliverance sessions. There may be some unusual thoughts or information that may come to mind. Team members take their thoughts captive and submit them to Jesus. If it is information that comes from the Holy Spirit, it will return. Sometimes they do this several times before using the information in deliverance. If only Christians would do this before saying, "Thus saith the Lord."

With the thought handed over to Jesus, let go and walk away.

The problem is we don't let go. We usually have a wrestling match with Jesus. It is difficult to let go of something that has been our truth for so long. Even though that core belief causes pain, it is familiar. The known pain appears to be more comforting than unfamiliar freedom. After all, if I let this core belief go, then the question of "Who am I?" is too scary.

This is why we do what we think is the spiritual thing to do: we pray for the Lord to take our painful emotions and problem behaviors away. We quote verses like "create in me a clean heart" and sing songs like "Refiner's Fire." This shows we do not know the nature of God.

God will never, never, ever, did I say N-E-V-E-R violate our will. He created us with a will and a choice. No one will ever be born again against his or her will. We choose what we believe. We have to surrender what we believe to Him. If we surrender, He will take it. As I previously stated, to surrender means for us to let go and walk away. Because of our difficulty with true surrender, sometimes this third Wholeness Step of Release— taking your thoughts captive—needs to be done again and again.

Caroline Leaf explains it takes 21 days to stop a thought and it takes 66 days to change it. This is how our brains physiologically function if we choose to change our minds. In the next chapter, I want to introduce you to the supernatural of the Kingdom and how God heals the wounded soul and actually changes the way we think.

SUMMARY OF TAKING THOUGHTS CAPTIVE:

Say, "Stop, in the name of Jesus!"
Say, "I take authority over this thought."
Take a moment to search and interrogate the thought.
Then say, "I bind you in the name of Jesus,"
and "I release you to Him."

The first three Wholeness Steps are crucial in the effective application of the last two steps. The first three steps are only the beginning of the process of repentance, changing the way you think. They open and prepare you to receive. Remember the parable of the soils? The first three steps break up the hard path and the stony ground and prepare it to receive the seed—the true seed.

Chapter 13

WHOLENESS STEP FOUR:
INVITE GOD'S PRESENCE

*The Lord is my Shepherd, I shall not be in want. He
makes me lie down in green pastures, he leads me
beside quiet waters, he restores my soul.*
Psalm 23:1-2

Two supernatural components of the Kingdom are available
to heal the wounded soul. King David recognized both of them.
Step Four is about God's presence. David loved being in God's
presence. He discovered God's power to heal the wounded soul
is in the presence of the Creator. The Psalms are his expressions
of worship (focusing on who God is) and experiencing His
divine presence: *"One thing I ask from the LORD, this only do I
seek: that I may dwell in the house of the LORD all the days of
my life, to gaze on the beauty of the LORD and to seek him in his
temple"* (Psalm 27:4).

Adam and Eve were created to live in God's presence.
They not only experienced God's love, they daily experienced
Him, the glory of His divine presence. They were one with the
Creator. They were complete and whole. Jesus came to restore
the presence of God to those who choose to follow Him. Jesus
declared in Luke 4:18 how He would restore the presence of

God, but first He had to pay the penalty for the sin of Adam and Eve and the rest of mankind. By His death and resurrection, He redeemed us. Then He left us His Holy Spirit to be the One who connects us to the Father.

The Holy Spirit is the One who heals and comforts our wounded soul. His Presence reveals to us the presence of *Jehovah Rapha*, the Lord who heals. The Lord expressed His nature in His name in Exodus 15:26: *"He said, 'If you listen carefully to the LORD your God and do what is right in his eyes, if you pay attention to his commands and keep all his decrees, I will not bring on you any of the diseases I brought on the Egyptians, for I am the LORD, who heals you.'"*

Because of our deeply rooted core belief, we don't believe in the ever-present Creator, *Jehovah Shammah*, the Lord who is there. This Fourth step is to acknowledge He is present and to allow His presence to be as *Jehovah Shalom*, the Lord my peace. A closer look at this name of God, *Jehovah Shalom*, is not about feeling peaceful in God's presence but about the true meaning of *shalom*. *Shalom* means "more than peace." It conveys feeling, intent, and emotion. It is a feeling of contentment, completeness, wholeness, well-being, and harmony. In Isaiah 9:6 Jesus is called the Prince of Peace: *"His names will be: Amazing Counselor, Strong God, Eternal Father, Prince of Wholeness. His ruling authority will grow, and there'll be no limits to the wholeness he brings"* (Isaiah 9:6, MSG).

I am referring to this step as an act of worship, and that "worship" is focusing on who God is. God inhabits the praises of His people. *"But thou art holy, O thou that inhabitest the praises of Israel"* (Psalm 22:3, KJV). As we acknowledge His presence, the eyes of our hearts are opened to Him.

In the book T*he Healing Presence: Curing the Soul Through Union with Christ*, Leanne Payne writes, "The practice of the Presence, then, is simply the discipline of calling to mind the truth that God is with us." She also quotes C.S. Lewis:

The presence of God is not the same as the sense of the presence of God. The latter may be due to imaginations; the former may be attended with no "sensible consolation." The act which engenders a child ought to be, and usually is attended by pleasure. But it is not the pleasure that produces the child. Where there is pleasure there may be sterility: where there is no pleasure the act may be fertile. And in the spiritual marriage of God and the soul it is the same. It is the actual presence, not the sensation of the presence of the Holy Ghost which begets Christ in us. The sense of the presence is a super-added gift for which we give thanks when it comes.

God's desire for us is more than accepting His presence by faith, but to experience Him and delight in His presence. Several places in scripture present us with experiencing the Presence:

In Your presence is fullness of joy...
Psalm 16:11, NKJV

That My joy may remain in you, and that your joy may be full...
John 15:11, NKJV

Abide in me, and I in you...
John 15:4a, KJV

But the fruit of the Spirit is love, joy, peace, patience, kindness, goodness, faithfulness, gentleness and self-control...
Galatians 5:22-23a

I have given them the glory that you gave me, that they may be one as we are one...
John 17:22

I have shared about the renewal meetings we attended in Florida. The presence of the Holy Spirit was experienced, and many Christians flocked to meetings like it as the movement spread throughout the country, as well as the world. Broken people looked—and are still looking—to experience God's presence. Why? Because we long to feel love, acceptance, a sense of belonging and well-being. What happens when we leave that experience of His presence? Ruled by our core beliefs, we go back to our default of pain and brokenness and our symptom behaviors. That is because we go into His presence unprepared by the first three Wholeness Steps. Those first three steps expose the festering wound containing our core belief and open the way for the presence to go deep into the wounded core, bringing His healing essence. The presence of the Lord of wholeness binds us in oneness with Himself as He provides our most basic human need: unconditional love. His love then defines us in the core of our being and transforms us "in the inmost place" where He implants His *truth* in Step Five.

This fourth step is simply then an act of worship. Focus on who God is. The Holy Spirit is our agent of healing. Jesus said He would not leave us comfortless but would send another Comforter, His Holy Spirit. The Holy Spirit only comforts where He is invited. Oftentimes we choose to suffer in our self-pity rather than allow the Holy Spirit into our wounded self.

In this step:

Ask by inviting the Holy Spirit into your wound.

Allow the Holy Spirit to connect you to the presence, the essence of God Himself, as healing love into your wounded place.

Accept His love and surrender any resistance to receiving His love. As you begin to sense His presence, even a small one at first, then you are ready to move on to the last step.

People tell me that in the beginning of learning these steps, they find this is the most difficult step: to allow themselves to be loved. This is because of core beliefs that say, "I am unworthy of love." If you are finding this step difficult, then go back to the beginning and start with that core belief, "I am unworthy of love," to bring God's healing to that wound. Then you will find this step will become easier to do. Eventually this step will be a part of your everyday Christian life, and finding and experiencing God's presence will be as easy as walking from one room into another.

Chapter 14

WHOLENESS STEP FIVE:
MAKE KINGDOM DECLARATIONS

*For the word of God is living and active. Sharper than
any double-edged sword, it penetrates even to dividing
soul and spirit, joints and marrow; it judges the
thoughts and attitudes of the heart.*
Hebrews 4:12

This last step is the other supernatural inner healing
component of the Kingdom: God's Word. **Ask God to speak a
declaration of who He is** into your core. This is asking God to
communicate with you. You will know when it is the Lord and
His words because it will be confirmed in the bible. John wrote
in 1 John 4:1a, *"Do not believe every spirit, but test the spirits to
see whether they are from God."* Do not believe everything you
think you hear spoken into your spirit. Look up in scripture what
you feel God is speaking to you. God's Word is written for us to
read and verify what He speaks into our souls. His spoken word
will identify Himself and His nature.

The Lord may speak a revelation into your soul right away,
but He may also wait for just the right time. This revelation of
His written Word is spoken into you to declare His identity as

Savior, Deliverer, Healer, Comforter, Provider. As He declares who He is, He is also declaring His relationship to you, which verifies your identity.

GOD'S DECLARATION

> *This is my beloved Son in whom I am well pleased.*
> Mathew 3:17, NKJV

When Jesus was baptized and came out of the water, what did He hear? God made a declaration over Jesus. Who was the focus of this declaration? God made a declaration **of Himself** over his Son. This is MY beloved son. 'I AM' is well pleased.

When making a Kingdom Declaration, you are asking God to make a declaration of Himself, over you. He wants to declare who He is into your broken, wounded, and weary soul. We have spent our lives trying to protect, comfort, and fix ourselves. (Remember our coping behaviors?) This last step is asking Father for a personal revelation of His identity.

Speak and declare His identity, giving power to His Word over you. His truth and His Word becomes the stronghold, the safe place of the restoration of your identity. *"The name of the Lord is a strong tower; the righteous run to it and are safe"* (Proverbs 18:10).

Then you can make Him your focus and declare: "You are my fortress. You are my high tower. You are my place of refuge and protection." Our comfort and healing come because of who He is, not because of who we are. Even Paul admitted he is the greatest of sinners and said, "There is no one righteous, no not one." It is God's presence, His nature, that heals us.

Many struggle with this step because this may sound completely foreign to what we are currently taught in present day Christianity about making positive self-affirmations.

THE FOCUS OF SELF-AFFIRMATION DECLARATIONS

Over the last 30 years, we have been inundated with teachings of positive self-affirmations from sources both inside and outside of the church. From self-improvement seminars to the current trends of many ministries, we hear that we are to declare how awesome we are. While we need to stop the negative self-talk coming from our core belief judgment, changing the way we speak is not the source of healing. When we declare things like "I am a child of the King! I can do all things through Him! I am the head and not the tail! I am... I am... I am..." Who is the focus of these declarations?

Ourselves.

When Paul declares his spiritual resumé in Philippians 3:4-8, he also says that he counts it as worthless for the cross of Christ. While we think that only pertains to his religious activity and standing before Christ, Paul concludes that he considers it as dung—yes, doo doo—as compared to the value of knowing Christ Jesus the Lord. Paul's focus is on knowing Christ, not on himself.

> *...for whom I have suffered the loss of all things, and do count them but dung, that I may win Christ.*
> Philippians 3:8b, KJV

Positive self-affirmations are limited in effectiveness to the upper 10% of our intellectual memory. It is a part of behavior modification which is only a minimal or even temporary means of change. Self-affirmation is like washing only the outside of a cup. Jesus said, *"Blind Pharisee! First clean the inside of the cup and dish, and then the outside also will be clean,"* (Matthew 23:6).

The focus of self-affirmation then becomes looking to ourselves to heal ourselves. In Luke 4:18, Jesus said that He came to heal the broken hearted. If we are looking to ourselves as the source of healing and comfort, we become our own mirror. We become our own source. We become our own god. God's first commandment to the children of Israel was, *"You shall have no other gods before me"* (Exodus 20:3). We need to look into the mirror of God's identity and declare who He is. Look to the Holy Spirit as our source of comfort and focus on Father's identity as our source of healing.

> *Come, let us tell of the LORD's greatness; let us exalt*
> *his name together. I prayed to the LORD, and he*
> *answered me. He freed me from all my fears.*
> Psalm 34:3-4, NLT

THE POWER OF OUR WORDS

Let me take a moment to say that we do need to stop the negative self-talk. It flows from the negative judgment of our core belief, our wounded soul. Proverbs 18:21 says that *"life and death is in the power of the tongue."* Our wounded, toxic souls produce the toxic fruit of negative words about ourselves. Knowingly or unknowingly, our negative self-talk works like a curse, speaking death to our spirit, soul, and even our bodies.

Words have power because they are sourced in what we believe.

> *A good tree can't produce bad fruit, and a bad tree*
> *can't produce good fruit. A tree is identified by the kind*
> *of fruit it produces. Figs never grow on thorn bushes*
> *or grapes on bramble bushes. A good person produces*
> *good deeds from a good heart, and an evil person*
> *produces evil deeds from an evil heart. Whatever is in*
> *your heart determines what you say.*
> Luke 6:43-45, NLT

Jesus said, "Repent," meaning change the way you think. On the diagram of the plant, whatever is at the root, determines the fruit. Have you ever said any of these negative statements? "I am so stupid." "I am so useless." "Nobody loves me." "I can't do anything right." "I am not good enough." "I am worthless."

We constantly curse, in agreement with our pain. When we speak these curses, they are kingly declarations. Now that our core beliefs are exposed in *The Five Wholeness Steps*, the fruit of our lips needs to change also. We need to stop cursing ourselves and stop the flow of toxic words. But doing *only* this isn't enough to heal us. We need God to heal the root of those toxins.

KINGDOM SUPERPOWER

Many ask if the core belief disappears or changes to a positive belief. As a physical wound heals, it gets smaller and smaller. It doesn't disappear, it becomes a scar. As you heal the wound in your soul, the strength of your core belief diminishes. Its power to rule becomes less and less. It will never completely disappear. That will only happen when we see Jesus face to face. Through His healing, these scars eventually become memories with no destructive, negative power.

Our core belief also does not change into a positive belief. Admitting the core belief of "I am powerless" means I am weak, and He is strong. We must admit that we have no righteousness, no strength of our own. Healing takes the power away from that core belief and gives the power back to God, and rightfully so. If we suddenly decide that we are strong, then we stop allowing Him to be the strength in our life.

Failure is the biggest commodity in the Kingdom. Our core belief becomes our Upside Down Kingdom superpower. Paul shows us the Kingdom value of our core belief:

> *I want to know Christ—yes, to know the power of*
> *his resurrection and participation in his sufferings,*
> *becoming like him in his death,*
> Philippians 3:10

When looked at upside down, what our earthly minds see as the least valuable becomes the most valuable thing about you. How can our core belief have value? The healing takes away the pain and negative power of the core belief. The transformation of our inner man is not changing us into super humans with no painful emotions of fear or anger. The transformation of our inner man is to embrace in our "in-most parts" God's belief about us. Admitting our failures and weaknesses is admitting we need God.

The Wholeness journey is one of empowerment to grasp how deep, how wide, how long is God's love (Ephesians 3:18). The process of transformation in our core will grow different fruit of behaviors, emotions, and thought patterns: the fruits of the Spirit. We heal to embrace God's love, grace, and forgiveness on a much deeper level. No longer limited to just intellectual knowledge, we experience liberty from the rule of the bruise and His healing presence is absorbed into our core, the inmost place.

THE POWER OF GOD-FOCUSED DECLARATIONS

All through the Psalms, David shows us the source of our healing and restoration. In Psalms 34:3-4 he declares, *"Oh magnify the Lord with me; let us exalt his name together. I sought the Lord, and he answered me; and delivered me from all my fears."* While deliverance from demons removes the enemy infiltration, David is talking about restoration from the fears in our core beliefs. Do we really believe in the Lord as our Shepherd (Psalm 23) who feeds us, guides us, heals us, watches over us, and protects us?

Our core beliefs have not only built *our* false identity, but also have built a false identity of *God*. Logically, if a core belief says that I am unworthy of love, then we do not believe that God loves us. If our core says that I am unworthy of value, then we do not believe that God values us. If we believe that we are not worthy of forgiveness, then we do not allow ourselves to accept His forgiveness. Instead we have lived under the rule of our core belief judgments as the source of our identity. God should be the source of our identity and healing. Let's declare who He is into our inmost being.

Surely you desire truth in the inner parts; you teach me
wisdom in the inmost place.
Psalm 51:6

Chapter 15

THE FIVE WHOLENESS STEPS
OVERVIEW

Pray *The Five Wholeness Steps* to apply God's healing presence into the wounded soul and bring transformation to the inner man.

Identify the Wound, the core belief (self-judgment) at the root of painful emotions and problem behaviors. Since birth, your identity and worldview have been based upon a lie rather than God's truth: *"As a man thinks in his heart, so is he"* (Proverbs 23:7).

Confess the Core Belief to Father, allowing Him to cleanse the wound. *"If we confess our sins* (our lies; faulty, negative, toxic, kingdom of darkness thinking), *he is faithful and just to forgive us our sins, and to cleanse us from all unrighteousness"* (1 John 1:9).

Hand it to Jesus. 2 Corinthians 10:5b says to *"bring into captivity every thought to the obedience of Christ."* Take authority and hand over the faulty thinking and beliefs to Jesus the way a policeman apprehends a suspect. Die as if your life depends on it (Galatians 2:20). 2 Corinthians 10:4 states you have the weapons (of life) to demolish the strongholds of thinking that are in opposition to the knowledge of God or oppose what God thinks.

Invite God's Presence. Invite the Holy Spirit to connect you to the presence of God, the supernatural healing component to heal the wounds of loss or offense where the lie was created and lives. Jesus declares in Luke 4:18 that He came to heal the broken heart and to liberate us from the bruises of life. As Jesus ascended after the resurrection, He said He would send a comforter. The Holy Spirit is our agent of healing, comforting the broken heart and transforming the mind as we practice His presence. Romans 12:1-2 describes mind renewing as an act of worship in which our minds are changed in His presence. Go into His presence and find His healing essence—love. Let His love heal you.

Make Kingdom Declarations to come into agreement with His truth and give power to His Word. Ask Father for a revelation of His truth: *"In Christ we find out who we are and what we are living for"* (Ephesians 1:11, MSG). *"God's Word is a two-edged sword dividing between the thoughts and intents of the heart"* (Hebrews 4:12). The Word of God works like a surgeon's scalpel to expose the darkness in our hearts and heal. Speak and declare who He is.

Paul sums up the process in this way:

I pray that out of his glorious riches, he may strengthen
you with power through his Spirit in your inner being,
so that Christ may dwell in your hearts through faith.
And I pray that you being rooted and established in
love, may have power together with all the saints, to

grasp how wide, and long and high and deep is the
love of Christ and to know this love that surpasses
knowledge –that you may be filled to the measure of the
fullness of God.
Ephesians 3:16-19

THE
FIVE
WHOLENESS STEPS

IDENTIFY the Wound

CONFESS the Core Belief

HAND it to Jesus

INVITE God's Presence

MAKE Kingdom Declarations

BCRcamp.com

This image maybe copied for personal use only.

Chapter 16

REAL LIFE, PRACTICAL APPLICATION

HEAL DAILY

Because we have been passively allowing the core belief to rule us, God's Truth was not allowed to take root. We are not properly applying the truth of God's Word. It's like getting a prescription of an antibiotic from the doctor to treat a strep throat infection. If you rub the bottle on your neck, is it going to work? No. It needs to be taken internally in order to apply it to the infection. Also, the doctor will tell you to take the full dosage to treat the infection until it is gone. That means you need to dose yourself with healing daily.

I love how each step of *The Five Wholeness Steps* spells "I. C. Him." *The Five Wholeness Steps* are a pattern of dialog and intimate interaction with Father, Son, and Holy Spirit. These steps guide us from our self-judgments, turn our focus to Him and His power to heal, and transform us.

The first three of *The Five Wholeness Steps* are our part—to open up and expose the wound, the core belief. The fourth step is God's part—we invite His presence, His essence, to pour supernatural healing into the wound. Just like a physical wound, it becomes smaller as it heals, and the power of the pain is diminished. In Step Five, we take our eyes off ourselves—stop protecting, fixing, and comforting ourselves—and turn our eyes to Him, bringing His truth into our inner parts. In this last step, the declaration of *who God is* can heal and restore us. Our comfort and healing come because of who He is, not because of who we are.

APPLICATION

If you cut your hand while cutting up vegetables in the kitchen, you wouldn't ignore the wound and bleed, would you? No. You have some idea of first aid and would tend to your wound. You'd first say something like, "Hey! I cut myself!" Then you would clean the wound, maybe put some ointment on it, and wrap it with a bandage. How much more do we need to apply God's healing to our wounds that show up every day?

I like things to be simple. I like practical. I want to know how I can apply biblical truths to my busy, everyday life. Although I recommend memorizing the steps, you have permission to make copies of the page with *The Five Wholeness Steps* so you can tape one to your bathroom mirror, put one on your refrigerator, and carry one with you.

Here is a practical example of how simple it is to apply *The Five Wholeness Steps* in everyday life.

A couple of years into my healing journey, Tim and I were at the local gym. I was on a machine doing an overhead lift workout. Tim was finished with what he was doing and came over to me and said, "You'd get a better workout if you did it correctly."

As we both looked at each other in the mirror on the wall, I replied, "Okay, thanks, Honey." As he walked away, I could feel the anger flames rising up in me.

Since I had worked on my stuff for some time, I knew better than to blame what I felt on Tim. Even though we want to blame our pain on what others say and do, I knew he was not the source of my pain. The true source of my pain was something unhealed in me. So I asked the Lord, "What is at the root of this response?"

While still doing my reps, a memory came to the surface. (A memory may surface to help identify a core belief, but not always. Sometimes there is no memory, only a feeling, or a knowing.) In this memory, I was at the piano. My mother was my piano teacher, so I had to have a lesson when she wanted me to have a lesson and practice when *she* wanted me to practice. She would hover over me and correct me. I would resist and talk back. I would be spanked or get my hands hit with a ruler.

Suddenly, in the midst of this memory, I realized I confused correction with punishment. Any time I was corrected, I felt punished. Because this memory involved my mother, I felt punished, rejected, abandoned, and insignificant. There it was, a core belief: "I am insignificant."

Identifying it was the first step. I quickly followed through with the next step of confession while continuing my overhead reps. I handed my self-judgment over to Jesus and then invited the Holy Spirit to pour the Father's healing love into my wounded soul. It didn't take long, and soon I felt liquid love flowing into the gaping wound. While still working out, with my eyes closed, I asked God to speak His healing truth into my soul.

Right away I felt I heard Him say, "Those I love, I discipline."

I responded to Him saying, "Lord, I don't want to reject your loving discipline."

I opened my eyes and realized where I was, in a gym, a place where we caringly discipline our bodies for our health and wellbeing. I thought to myself, "Nice one, Lord."

The Five Wholeness Steps take only a few minutes, but their impact is extensive. Every one of the Five Steps is powerful in and of itself: identification, confession, taking thoughts captive, the presence, and His Word. When combined, there is a synergistic Kingdom power released into the deeply wounded, hidden place. Bombarding the wound with His healing presence transforms the soul. It changes the way you think and what you believe from that kingdom of darkness identity to carrying it in the inmost part His truth about who you are.

How would your life be different if you believed in the core of your being that you were fully loved and valued by your Creator Father? What if you had access to all the riches of the Kingdom because of your identity of being one with Him? Sometimes people tell me that they already know it. I ask them, "If what you say is true, then where are the miracles and the supernatural manifestations of the Kingdom?" Because of Jesus' true identity, He did what He saw His Father do. He was in this natural realm, but not limited to the laws of the natural realm.

If we have this true identity in the core of our being, we will experience the Kingdom of light too. The healing journey doesn't end until we see Him face to face. Then we will be ultimately transformed. We will be like Him, and we will see Him as He is. That is why I still pursue Him. It's all about less of me and more of Him.

INTRODUCING THE HEALING PATH WORKBOOK

I have written *The Healing Path* as a supplement to this book. It is a workbook to guide you in learning how to recognize core beliefs and how to apply healing through *The Five Wholeness Steps* over a four-week period. The manual and audio CD will assist you in implanting God's healing, and you will experience Him and His transforming presence.

In the early days right after my deliverance, I had to slow my busy life down and commit the time to focus on pursuing healing and allow myself to heal. Although painful, I had to spend the time exposing the wounds and surrendering them to Father. It was difficult because I did not have anyone to tell me that I would be okay. You have these materials to guide you and encourage you. Nobody told me that eventually the pain in my soul would subside and a love would emerge. Nobody was there to tell me that I would be redeemed and transformed, nobody except the Father, when He told me through Tim, "As a reminder of the mighty thing that I'm going to do, call her Katie."

I am here to tell you through my story in these pages that as long as you give yourself to His healing, *you will change.* The pain in your soul will subside. Most of all, you will find what your soul craves. His love will heal you. His presence will transform you. You will experience Him and see for yourself that as you gaze upon Him, in the glory of His essence, you will find you are the twinkle in His eye.

ACKNOWLEDGMENTS

Thank you, Tim, for comforting me with the affirmation that writing a book is a difficult task. You are so patient with struggling beginners. Thanks for giving me the time, space, prodding, and encouragement.

To David Dudley, thank you for taking the time to edit this manuscript. You're not just a friend, but also a valuable part of this ministry.

For our intercessors, a big thank you. Your prayers keep us going.

To those who support us financially, your generous giving makes ministry possible to folks all over the United States and around the world.

Thank you to my daughter, Heather, and her husband, Kevin. Since you joined us full-time, you have made it possible for me to write instead of cook, clean, serve, paint, and administrate.

For all my children and their spouses, Erin and Jason, Lucas and Pam, and Amber and Justin: thank you for the interventions where you confronted me to write. You are my motivation to pass this revelation on and for you to pass it on to your children and your grandchildren. I love to watch your lives. I am blessed by your love and pursuit of God.

ABOUT THE AUTHOR

Katie Mather is an author, conference speaker, and Wholeness Coach. She holds a BS in Pastoral Counseling from Oral Roberts University and a Doctor of Ministry from Covenant Bible Institute. She and her husband, Tim, host Deliverance and Advanced Wholeness Retreats at Bear Creek Ranch in North Georgia. They have fifteen (and counting) grandchildren and four married children, many of whom help staff the retreats.

WORKS CITED

Barna, George. Barna Survey Examines Changes in Worldview Among Christians over the Past 13 Years. Barna. com. Barna Group. 6 March 2009. Web. 12August2015. https://www.barna.com/research/barna-survey-examines-changes-in-worldview-among-christians-over-the-past-13-years/

Bible, The Holy. New International Version (Grand Rapids, MI: 1973).

Bible, The Holy. King James Version (USA: Thomas Nelson Publishers, 1972).

Bible, The Holy. New King James Version, (USA: Thomas Nelson Publishers, 2007).

"Eleven Facts About Global Poverty." DoSomething. org. Web. 12 August 2015. https://www.dosomething.org/tipsandtools/11-facts-about-global-poverty

Gaither, William J. He Touched Me, (Gaither Music, 1963).

Hadhazy, Adam. "Think Twice: How the Gut's 'Second Brain' Influences Mood and Well-being." Scientific American. com. 12 February 2010. Web. 12August2015. http://www.scientificamerican.com/article/gut-second-brain/

Johnson, David and VanVonderen, Jeff. The Subtle Power of Spiritual Abuse, (Minneapolis, Minnesota: Bethany House Publishers, 1991).

Kubetin, Cindy. Beyond the Darkness, (Dallas, TX: Rapha Publishing, 1992).

Leaf, Dr. Caroline. Who Switched Off My Brain? (USA: Switch on Your Brain Organization, 2002).

Lewis, C. S. Letters to an American Lady, ed. Clyde S. Kilby (Grand Rapids, MI: Eerdmans, 1967), pp 36-37.

Loyd, Dr. Alexander. The Healing Code, (New York, New York: Grand Central Publishing, 2010).

Mather, Tim. Out of Bondage, (USA: BCR Press, 2017).

Mather, Tim. Prophetic Deliverance, (USA: BCR Press, 2018).

McGee, Robert S. The Search for Reality, (USA: McGee and Me Publishing, 2014).

McGee, Robert S. The Search for Significance, (Nashville, Tennessee: Word Publishing, 1998).

Payne, Leanne. The Healing Presence, (USA: Hamewith Books, 2001).

Peterson, Eugene H. The Message Bible (Colorado Springs, CO: Alive Communications, Inc., 2002).

Richards, Dr. James B. How to Stop the Pain, (New Kensington, Pennsylvania: Whitaker House, 2001).

Seamands, David A. Healing for Damaged Emotions, (New York: Inspirational Press, 1993).

Seamands, David A. Putting Away Childish Things, (New York: Inspirational Press, 1993).

Seamands, David A. Healing of Memories, (New York: Inspirational Press, 1993).

Seamands, David A. Freedom from the Performance Trap, (New York: Inspirational Press, 1993).

"The Meaning of the Word, Shalom." TheRefiner'sFire. com. Web. 12 August 2015. http://www.therefinersfire.org/meaning_of_shalom.htm

BEAR CREEK RANCH

Deliverance & Wholeness Retreats

Pursuing inner healing before deliverance is like putting the cart before the horse.

Jesus' mission statement in Luke 4: 18-19 KJV includes the six supernatural elements of life in Christ: discovery of the good news of Kingdom life, healing for the brokenness, freedom from demonic influences, new spiritual sight, liberty from Kingdom of Darkness thinking and the revelation that we are now Father's favorite. None of them are automatic upon entrance to the Kingdom of Light. Rather, the revelations must be pursued, the healing apprehended, the sight revealed. Therefore, each and every person making their way into the Kingdom needs deliverance.

Read *Prophetic Deliverance* by Tim Mather for an up-close view of this tool for freedom from demonization.

Tim and Katie Mather seek to provide a place for people to come and receive the ministry of Deliverance and Inner Healing, through seminars and workshops at Bear Creek Ranch.

Visit www.BCRcamp.com for retreat information.

RESOURCES

BOOKS:

Prophetic Deliverance
by Tim Mather

Escaping Church
by Tim Mather

Out of Bondage
by Tim Mather

Supernatural Superheroes
by Heather Trim

AUDIO TEACHINGS:

**Upside Down
Kingdom Weapons**
with Tim Mather

Wholeness JumpStart
with Katie Mather

Visit the Bear Creek Bookstore for more information.
www.BCRcamp.com

Workbook

A GUIDE TO WHOLENESS THROUGH INNER HEALING

Katie Mather

CPSIA information can be obtained
at www.ICGtesting.com
Printed in the USA
LVHW110011080420
652594LV00005B/1619